Backstory

AVANI GREGG

Backstory

My Life So Far

G

GALLERY BOOKS

New York   London   Toronto   Sydney   New Delhi

G

Gallery Books
An Imprint of Simon & Schuster, Inc.
1230 Avenue of the Americas
New York, NY 10020

First Gallery Books hardcover edition September 2021

GALLERY BOOKS and colophon are registered trademarks
of Simon & Schuster, Inc.

For information about special discounts for bulk purchases,
please contact Simon & Schuster Special Sales at 1-866-506-1949
or business@simonandschuster.com.

The Simon & Schuster Speakers Bureau can bring authors
to your live event. For more information or to book an event,
contact the Simon & Schuster Speakers Bureau at 1-866-248-3049
or visit our website at www.simonspeakers.com.

Interior design by Davina Mock-Maniscalco

Manufactured in the United States of America

10   9   8   7   6   5   4   3   2   1

Library of Congress Cataloging-in-Publication Data

Names: Gregg, Avani, 2002– author.
Title: Backstory : my life so far / Avani Gregg.
Description: First Gallery Books hardcover edition. | New York : Gallery
   Books, 2021.
Identifiers: LCCN 2021021640 (print) | LCCN 2021021641 (ebook) | ISBN
   9781982171575 (hardcover) | ISBN 9781982171582 (trade paperback) |
   ISBN 9781982171599 (ebook)
Subjects: LCSH: Gregg, Avani, 2002– | Internet personalities—United
   States—Biography. | TikTok (Electronic resource) | Actors—United States—
   Biography. | LCGFT: Autobiographies.
Classification: LCC PN1992.9236.G74 A25 2021 (print) | LCC
   PN1992.9236.G74 (ebook) | DDC 818/.603 [B]—dc23
LC record available at https://lccn.loc.gov/2021021640
LC ebook record available at https://lccn.loc.gov/2021021641

ISBN 978-1-9821-7157-5
ISBN 978-1-9821-7159-9 (ebook)

To my family and friends,
who helped me get through all my ups and downs
(and also went through ups and downs because of me).

contents

introduction

Hey, Bebs!

*S*o, this is me, writing a book. Never thought I'd say those words (school essays aren't my favorite thing), but here I am. People think they know me because I post thirty-second videos vibing on social media. But I guarantee you they don't know the backstory—not even half of it. Just because you see me on Tik-Tok doesn't mean you know what makes me tick or who Clown Girl really is when the makeup comes off.

Why? For a long time, I wasn't ready to tell you. I'm not someone who likes to spill the tea. TBH, I'm a little guarded and it takes a lot to break down my walls. But 2020 propelled me into a new place and got me thinking, *Shouldn't we all know each other's backstory? Wouldn't it help us understand each other more and treat each other better?* Because honestly, the world is not a happy, carefree place at the moment, despite all the fun and games you see on social media. There is a lot of ugliness, hate, and misunderstanding out there, and that was before we were cooped up inside thanks to the pandemic. As someone who has a public platform, I feel like I should do my part to put some of that toxicity to rest. That's why I post videos and images, and it's why I started my Messenger Watch Together show,

Here For It with Avani Gregg. I wanted to start a conversation so we could all learn a little more about ourselves and connect with one another. I want this book to do the same—to open eyes and set wheels in motion. There's a lot of stuff we all think and feel but are afraid to say out loud. Well, I'm saying it, and trigger warning: it's gonna get deep.

You might think my life has been picture-perfect (social media would have you think so, right?), but that's a lie. Like everyone, I've been through pain, loss, hate, and bad days as well as good ones. I've struggled and I continue to struggle, but I've learned you can bounce back from adversity better and stronger. You start by surrounding yourself with people who genuinely love and care about you (my "Team Avani"). Then you take a deep breath and start to connect the dots of your life. In my case, I wanted to start with my mom, my dad, and their roots, and take stock of everything that has happened in my eighteen years. Eighteen is a big birthday, and it seemed like a good time to reflect. I feel like I'm the same person, even if my daily life has changed dramatically from being a competitive gymnast to becoming known on social media. When I sat down to write this book, it was the beginning of the pandemic, so my head was in a weird place. I just wanted to be around my family and my boyfriend and shut the rest of the world out. I needed to feel safe and supported while my mental health was shaky. I needed to give myself some me time to *be* instead of *do*.

Somehow, putting words and emotions down on paper made me feel free; instead of hiding my backstory, I embraced it. I've been through a lot, but I also learned some important life lessons along the way. Not the things they teach you in school, but the real personal stuff you can *actually* use, like how to build your confidence, how to tune out negativity, and what to do when life throws you a curveball. I'll share what I've learned because, hey, we're all in this together, right? Hopefully, you can relate to my stories of toxic relationships, being bullied, falling on my face, and freaking out. I guess what I want you to know is that you're never alone in what you're going through. Your story is your story, but we have all been through stuff.

Still, even if I could go back and change anything, I don't think I would. Everything I've been through has shaped me into who I am today. I think you need to embrace your backstory so you can move forward—which is what I'm doing with this book. I have a lot of dreams and if I can own who I am, then I'll be that much closer to making them happen. Being real with yourself is what turns dreams into reality. I'm not a "fake it till you make it" person. I think authenticity is everything and when you're happy with yourself, no one can take that away from you. Your backstory is your superpower.

I started using the word "backstory" about a year ago, and it just stuck. You've probably seen it in some of my captions or heard me mention it in interviews. It gave both my work and my life a sense of purpose and clarity. It's the foundation that I build upon: everything happens for a reason and every choice you make is based on what came before it. I truly believe that everything and everyone has a backstory that colors who they are and how they see the world, and we should all try to understand each other on a deeper level. You never know what's going on in somebody's head—what's motivating them or holding them back. You can't, until you learn where they came from and how they arrived at where they are. Even then, you're not living in their skin. You're you, I'm me, and no two people are

100 percent alike. That's what makes the world such an amazing and interesting place.

What I want everyone to know is that I'm human, despite having more than 30 million followers on TikTok and more than 16 million on Instagram. If I've kept some things to myself, it's because my whole life is so "out there" for everyone to see, that I needed to tuck away a few things that were just mine. But I'm ready to let you in, and doing that comes with a lot of nerves as well as a big sigh of relief. Initially, I'm always afraid people will judge, but then I tell myself, "Let them." Bring it on. I'm just doing me and trying to be the happiest I can be.

Not everything I keep to myself is super serious. I have little quirks and pet peeves that only my closest friends and family know about. For example:

+ I won't do my homework until my mom tells me to. She will literally storm into my room to ask if it's done, and I shrug. "Nope, I didn't do it. You didn't remind me, so it's your fault!" She gets annoyed, and I crack up—I just love pushing her buttons!

+ I'm addicted to Diet Coke. All my friends love coffee, but when I wake up, I want my Diet Coke fix. My friends and I go to different fast-food places to see who has the best fountain Diet Coke. So far it's McDonald's, where it's always ice-cold and crispy-bubbly. I am very, very particular. One time, when I was fourteen, my dad took me to McDonald's and they accidentally gave me a Dr Pepper. When I sipped it, I actually started crying, so my dad turned around and went back to get me the right soda. You can't fool me—these taste buds know.

✦ I'm a night owl. I could stay up until five in the morning and not feel tired at all. I have to force myself to sleep. Then I wake up really late—like in time to eat dinner. It's totally fine by me if my day is upside down and I never see the sun. I might have been a vampire in another life.

✦ I don't like surprises or when unexpected things pop up in my schedule—I need to know what's happening every hour, every minute. When it comes to work and school, if things aren't planned, I get upset. I don't like to be spontaneous unless it's with my friends and we decide to go out somewhere. Otherwise, it better be on my Google Calendar so I can plan around it.

So yeah, that's me—the SparkNotes version! You'll have to dive into the following pages to learn the rest. What I hope you take away from them is this: things aren't always what they seem. There is so much more to me than what you see in a video or a feed post, and I'm ready to let you inside my head and my heart. I'm weird, I have flaws, I screw up, and I get frustrated, sad, and mad—sometimes all at once! It's crazy to me that people just don't understand that social media is a job that takes motivation, time, and a toll on my mental health. Yes, I'm really lucky to be up there at the top, but that doesn't mean my life is perfect. I'm also anxious and awkward, and there are days when I don't want to get out of bed. What keeps me motivated is the fact that I'm a creative person who needs to express herself, and I'm trying to figure out the best way to do that. It's also you—the people who follow me. You lift me up, and your love and support mean everything. Besides, I could never go back to my life before TikTok, even if I wanted to—too much time has passed and I don't really know how to live any other way. Before any of this happened, before I moved to LA and joined the Hype House, I was just this kid who went to school in Indiana. To be honest, I never saw any of it coming. But once it did, I had to figure out how to deal and what would come next.

Now I'm embracing my backstory and writing the next chapters (yeah, I just made a book pun). I'm excited to see what they hold. I hope you are, too!

ILY,

chapter one

Meet the Fam

I owe a lot of who I am to my parents—my sense of self and purpose, and my stubborn streak . . . yeah, I get it all from them. My fierce loyalty to the people I love? They're responsible for that, too. My cheesy, romantic view that one day you find your bae and live happily ever after? You guessed it. They instilled all of the above in me, through their words and actions. In fact, if you think about it, it's pretty funny that a social media influencer was so influenced by her mom and dad, but I gotta give them both creds. I would not be where I am today if it weren't for them.

My mom, Anisha, was a nurse for twenty-four years and my dad, Lewis, was a firefighter for thirteen years, so they both dedicated themselves to helping others. Neither of them has a selfish bone in their body; they are givers with all their heart and soul, freely and regardless of their own personal sacrifice. They come from very different backgrounds—my mom is Asian Indian, while my dad is part Mongolian and part African American. But they found each other and stuck it out for twenty-eight years now (first as friends, then as a couple) because they knew, just knew, that they were meant to be together. I know that sounds like a Netflix rom-com or something, but it wasn't all sunshine and roses. My parents didn't have an easy time of it. They knew that if they got married, it wouldn't be a stress-free, charmed life. My mom's parents had plans for her to have an arranged marriage, so my mom and dad knew that entering into a life together without a lot of family support, financially and otherwise, was going to be hard. They would struggle, not just to provide for our family, but also to make time for each other and figure out how to make things work. Still, they didn't hesitate, not for a second. They believed in love above all else—and you can roll your eyes, but I am a sucker for that kind of romance.

Their journey to finding each other was, well, let's just say complicated. My dad's dad (Lewis Sr., known as "Pop-Pop") was an MP (military policeman) in the army, and he was serving in the war over in Korea. From what I hear, he was a badass, and his job was to keep the peace with law enforcement and military authorities abroad. The way the story goes, he was at the end of his shift one night, hanging out with a friend, when he met a local girl in a village that was close to the army base. They hit it off, and soon after, he called his father back in the U.S. to ask for his blessing for marriage. My great-grandpa John told Pop-Pop to come back home and think about it. Translation: you are way too young to be talking marriage; come back to the States and you'll forget all about this girl. After all, Pop-Pop was only twenty at the time. Well, I guess stubborn really does run in the genes, because he reenlisted, extended his time over there, and married her anyway. Eventually, Pop-Pop came back and brought her with him, introducing her to the other military wives and families on his army base in Fort Hood, Texas. But she wasn't very happy. Between his job and several different sports teams,

Pop-Pop was gone all the time. My dad was just a baby, but Pop-Pop took him to all his practices and games, leaving his wife at home by herself. She quickly figured out this wasn't the life she signed up for, so she packed up and left and they later divorced. My dad stayed with Pop-Pop, but it didn't take long for everyone to realize that raising a toddler as a single parent in the military would be very hard to do. Pop-Pop's sister Justina, or "Mom-Mom," lived in Edgewood, Maryland, and agreed to take my dad in when he was two, to help raise him and provide a more stable environment.

My dad grew up thinking that Mom-Mom was his mom and his two older cousins, Tara and Melodye, were his sisters. It was really weird, this big secret they kept from him. He was about eight when they finally filled him in. He was a straight-A student and bookworm, and the news sent him spiraling. He says it "broke" him. Suddenly, nothing seemed to matter. He became rebellious and reckless, running with the wrong crowd and shoplifting. He was good at it, so he didn't get caught, which only made him want to get into more mischief. He was young, so he didn't know what was causing all these feelings or making him do these things, but looking back, he says it was all about anger and hurt. He felt betrayed and lied to, and I can only imagine how all that messed with his head. What would it feel like to have the rug pulled out from under you like that? It made him flip a switch: If they weren't his parents, why should he answer to them? Why should he listen to anyone?

In the meantime, Pop-Pop married his new wife, Janice, who had four kids from a prior marriage: Jimmy, Lori, Chrissy, and Johnny. When my dad was twelve, Pop-Pop came down to get him and bring him back to live in Indiana with his step-family. I guess he wanted to make things right between them, maybe fix my dad's bad 'tude. It wasn't exactly the happy homecoming my dad had imagined: the whole family stayed in a small four-bedroom town house. After that summer, my dad decided it wasn't for him; it was close quarters with people he barely knew. So he got on a Greyhound bus and went back to Maryland, where he had his own room and a family who took good care of him—even if Mom-Mom and Uncle Jimmy weren't his birth family. Three months later, my dad realized that he needed to be with Pop-Pop and moved back to Indiana once again. He says for the majority of his teen years, he was a pain in the butt, a "bad boy" who got kicked out of high school and then alternative school but eventually graduated after attending night school. It wasn't until he was about my age, eighteen, that he started to "straighten up." His family didn't have a lot of money back then, but they had a lot of love for each other, and that's all that really mattered. They made him feel included and a part of their lives.

Right after graduation, my dad moved out on his own, enrolled in college, joined the volunteer fire department for two years, and then pushed on to become a professional firefighter. "Nobody handed me nothing, Voni," he likes to remind me. "Everything I got, everything I am, I worked for."

You can see where I get my work ethic from—my dad taught me that nothing feels as good as something you've earned all by yourself. This is what Pop-Pop and Mom-Mom instilled in him, and he passed it on to me. Growing up, my sisters and I got an allowance after completing our chores, and if I wanted something, I had to pay for it. I worked on weekends and during the summers and wore Shanti's hand-me-downs from our older cousins. When they were too small for me, they went to Priya. So when people comment on my videos, calling me "rich" and "spoiled," I fire back. That couldn't be further from the truth. My dad is a proud, self-made man and living proof that you don't ever have to accept the cards you're dealt. You would never picture him as a rebellious kid, because he's so chill and laid-back now. He rarely cusses and he has the biggest, kindest, most generous heart. He never says no to any of us. He likes to go for long walks in nature and is always after me to get out more. I'm not really the "outdoorsy" type, but he reminds me how important it is to appreciate what's right under your nose. I don't know if he would have ever felt this way if his life had been easier or more "normal." He owns his past in a way that inspires me to do so too, because he is so open and honest about it. Sometimes I wonder where that courage comes from, but then I remember he used to fight fires for a living—he's not afraid of being burned.

My mom's backstory is very different. She was born in India and came to America when she was four. Her parents, Harkant and Kusum Patel, were immigrants who settled in Indiana. My mom has one older sister, Hemali, and one younger brother, Amar, who was born here. In Indian families, five is a small household—the usual is closer to half a dozen or more relatives under one roof. My mom's side of the family is huge, and she has tons of cousins, aunts, and uncles who are all very into their Indian faith and traditions. She and her siblings struggled at times with their new life in America—they wanted to celebrate all of the American holidays and just fit in and feel like they belonged here. When you're a kid, the last thing you want to be is different, but they couldn't help it. My mom's parents were Hindus and insisted the family be Indian to the core. They were really strict, and their main priority was for their kids to have a good education. My mom says her parents expected so much of her: she needed to go to college, get a degree, and of course, follow Indian traditions *or else*. When it came time for my mom to get married, her parents were determined to arrange it because, *hello*, that's what traditional Indian parents did back then. My mom's sister, Hemali, had an arranged marriage, and that's what my grandparents had in store for my mom as well. But she stood her ground: "Nope, not gonna happen."

My mom wanted to find a husband on her own time and terms. How could anyone else make that choice for her? She refused to even think about it and focused on her college courses until, one day, she met my dad. At the time, they were both dating other people, but they all would hang out together. When things didn't work out with their current relationships, my dad took his shot and pursued my mom. They hit it off and dated all through college. My mom kept putting off getting super serious with my dad because she had her mind set on completing nursing school. In the back of her mind, I think she knew that marrying my father meant that her parents would cut her off and even possibly disown her, so she had to be ready to pay her own way. She wasn't wrong: they were furious! My grandparents didn't want her to be with my dad, so my parents got married in a courthouse instead of having a big wedding. Yup, no reception, no one hundred–plus guests showering them with best wishes and gifts. It was . . . sad.

After they exchanged vows, my parents really didn't have any close communication with her parents for about a year. They settled into their home in Broad Ripple and then, about a year later, my mom got pregnant with my older sister, Shanti. That's when everyone decided to just forgive and forget—a grandchild was reason enough and, to this day, we're all really close to my grandparents. Even crazier? They love, love, love my dad! They saw what an amazing father he was and all their doubts and fears just flew out the window. When I ask my mom if all this drama was upsetting, she shrugs. "Voni," she tells me, "we're just not the norm. We don't follow what everyone else does." By "we" she means herself and my dad, but also me. She always tells me to blaze my own trail, ignore trends, and shake things up if need be. She believes strongly that you should do what makes you happy, even if it's not what everybody else is doing. In her case, that meant bending the rules when it came to her culture. Yes, she loves Indian food, clothes, and traditional holidays. But she didn't agree so much with the whole male-dominant culture and beliefs. What did you expect? She has three girls and she raised us to be strong, to be independent, and to know our worth.

Lucky for us, my dad is a great guy. He even resigned from the fire department and stayed home with us full-time while my mom went to work because her job had better pay and benefits. I think that's pretty amazing. You won't find a lot of guys eager to change diapers and go to Mommy and Me classes, but Dad never complained. He didn't care what anyone would think or say about it. To him, there was no greater job than caring for his girls and he didn't trust anyone else to do it.

I've had a great upbringing. I'm not "this" or "that" but a mix of many cultures, and my family embraces all of them. My mom and dad have always been so forthcoming about who they are and where they come from, and it gives me a unique perspective on the world. I know they told us a lot of this stuff when we were growing up, but none of it really resonated until now. I see the struggles they went through as the foundation for how they raised us. Their backstories color mine. I have a good life, a comfortable life, so I can't totally relate to the hardships they went through, but I do appreciate how they built themselves up and found each other along the way. I also realize how much they have done and continue to do for me. Beyond all the gymnastics meets, homework help, and plain ol' putting a roof over my head, they are my safety net. My mom has worked in the pharma industry for the past seventeen years, but she recently quit her job to help me with my career full-time. Some eighteen-year-olds would resent a parent being so involved, but I wouldn't want it any other way. She's got my back more than anyone. And my dad, well, he would move mountains for me. After all, he gave up his career in the fire department to take care of me and my sisters when we were little. But it's also the day-to-day stuff he does that means so much—silly things that he knows will put a smile on my face. I will never forget the time I went to Target at Halloween in search of this cute little light-up ghost decoration and they were out of them. I came home so upset and disappointed (yeah, I can be a bit of a drama queen). The next day, my dad snuck out and went to another Target further away to find one to surprise me. If that doesn't sum it up, I don't know what does: How many fathers would go "ghost hunting" just to make their kid happy?

I know I can be a handful sometimes, and my career doesn't make things particularly easy on my family. Our lives look very different than they did just a few years ago. My life has exploded, and I've gotten to travel the world and meet some really cool people. But on the other hand, Priya had to leave her friends in Indiana to move to LA, and Shanti has experienced the dark side of social media (people hating) because of me. My mom and dad hold it all together for us, no matter how much chaos is going down. But I do worry that I put my family through a lot because of the path I've chosen—and is that really fair? If you ask them, they'll say, "We're all in this together." And they're not just quoting the *High School Musical* anthem, they actually mean it. We are all feeling, and dealing with, the impact of me getting "famous." When I started blowing up, friends and strangers would try to use my sisters to get to me. When I would come to pick Priya up at school, they would surround the car. Or they'd follow Shanti on social media to try and get closer to me. But the one thing I really couldn't stand was when my sisters started getting hate on their own social media accounts. It was like my haters took it out on them— guilty by association. I don't care if they come after me, but my family did nothing to be on the receiving end of this . . . It makes me furious and I'm gonna clap back.

My mom is annoyingly practical about it all: "Do you enjoy what you're doing? Then stop reading the comments!" She's kinda right. She was also very insistent that if I was going to go into social media as a career, I had to do it the right way. "Is this what you want to pursue? Because if it is, you're not just going to move out to LA and go do your thing. We will all move, we will set you up with the right team, and you will still finish school." She does have a way of spelling things out—no ifs, ands, or buts about it! At the same time, she and Dad always let me chase my dreams. My dad is a dreamer like me, so he will tell me I can do anything I set my mind to. Did I mention he sees the word "impossible" as "I'm possible"? My mom will say, "Go for it," but then she will make sure I have a plan in place to see it through. She's the more realistic, detail-oriented person. I need both of them behind me because I have seen way too much crazy go down in this business. I know how easy it is to get taken advantage of, to feel intimidated by people who are older, more experienced, and convinced they know what's best for you. Spoiler alert: they don't. That's where my parents come in—my eyes, my ears, and my mouthpiece. If I am not happy, if I feel uncomfortable or disrespected, they will do whatever they need to do to make it right.

Are they a little overprotective sometimes? Um, yes. But then again, worrying *is* part of their job description. I know that above all else, they want me to be happy and trust my instincts. They know that they have to let me try, succeed, fail, and figure it out for myself. But even though they raised me to be independent, they want me to know I'm not flying solo. Especially during the pandemic, I had to constantly think about not just what *I* wanted, but also what was safe for the people I live with. It wasn't all about me; I had to consider how my actions would affect my family, and that helped me make smarter decisions for us all. You can call it a pod, a group, a tribe, whatever; for me, family is a reminder that I'm a part of something bigger than myself. That comes with responsibility, but it also comes with an incredible sense of belonging and security. I am not—and will never be—alone.

People ask who I'm more like, my mom or my dad. Hmmm, that's a tough one. The way I see it, I inherited qualities from each of them that blend well with my unique Avaniness. It's like my secret sauce: I have Mom's strength, laser-beam focus, and drive, and I have Dad's soft-spoken way and crazy, stupid love for people. When you mix it all together, you get me! They're also pretty cool and not too bossy, which we all know is a common parental trait. They try not to tell me what to do and let me handle my biz. Even if they're anxious over something— like one of the songs on my TikTok being too "raunchy"—they will offer words of wisdom, step aside, and hope that something they've said eventually sinks in. I'm gonna do what I'm gonna do, but if they nag me enough, some of it is bound to stick. Plus, they often have a very good point that's worth remembering or even writing down.

Let's just keep that between us. I don't need it goin' to their heads. ☺

Meet My Dogs!

*J*ack and Benny came into our lives in 2011, and they are just as much a part of our fam as I am. Of course, they have their own backstory. Our neighbor had a cute little Maltese dog that was rescued from an illegal puppy mill. They found out that this little dog was pregnant, and she eventually gave birth to a litter of five puppies. We don't know if they were mixed or purebred Maltese since the mom was a rescue, but what we do know is that they had a lot of health issues. When our neighbor's dog had the puppies, we decided that we would go and adopt one for our family. We had lost our Rottweiler, King, a couple of years earlier when we put him down due to cancer, and it left a big hole in all our hearts. Personally, I had been begging for another dog for a long time. When we went to choose one of the pups, my sisters and I fell in love with the runt of the litter. He had a blue collar on. Then there was this little butterball pup that kept coming up to us while the others shied away. He had a black collar on. We fell in love with both of them, so we ended up leaving with two puppies instead of one—a puppy jackpot! Our parents agreed to it because they thought it would be better to have a pair so they could keep each other company. We just couldn't choose between them.

My mom wanted to name them Ben and Jerry, like the ice cream, because who doesn't love ice cream? We all thought it was a cute idea . . . except Dad. So we compromised and went with Benny Blue and Jack Black, like the actor. They have been inseparable ever since. Every time they lie down, their bodies have to be touching. It's so adorable. I can't imagine my life without these little fur babies.

Run It Back:
Family Ties

*I*n case you missed it (or need a little cheat sheet), every chapter ends with my quick take on each topic. I don't know about you, but I like to have things summed up in a few short and sweet bullet points to keep on hand. I have a pretty bad memory (probs because I'm always doing five things at the same time), so the more you remind me of something, the better it sticks. Feel free to refer back to these boxes whenever you want to Krazy Glue a little inspo to your brain. You're welcome!

✦ The most important things in life aren't things, they're people. In my case, the fam I was born into and the one I choose (aka my friends and boyfriend) always come first.

✦ Family doesn't always have to be blood—it can be your beb or your bestie, a coach or a teacher, or another relative (like my mom-mom) who is there for you.

✦ Family will show up when you need them, to listen to you whine or wig out, to hug it out, or to make a midnight run to Mickey D's (okay, that might only be a few of you, but you know who you are).

+ Family will love you unconditionally, even if you mess up, complain, yell, order them out of your room, etc. You cannot kick them to the curb even if you try because they see through your nasty and know you are 110 percent awesome. You cannot convince them otherwise.

+ Family will tell it to you straight. It may not be what you want to hear, but it's almost always what you *need* to hear. So, listen. Be respectful. Let it sink in before you push it aside. Parents especially have an annoying habit of being right most of the time.

+ Your family's backstory colors yours. Even if that story is a little problematic (like my dad's), you can learn and grow from it. You can repeat the same mistakes, or you can do better. It's your choice.

+ Family is a reminder that you are part of something bigger than yourself. It's a community, no matter how big or small, and the people you consider your fam will always be your home.

On Avani

My inner circle is tight. These are the people who know me better than anyone, and I asked them to share memories of me in each chapter. I'm a little nervous for them to spill too much tea, but I told them not to hold back. I asked, "What's *your* Avani back-story?" and they all were eager to answer. Go ahead, guys, tell me what you *really* think!

My dad, Lewis Gregg, says:

I'm so proud of Avani and all she's accomplished, and I know it's just the beginning of what I like to call her "empire." She builds it with all this creativity and de-termination. I can truly say she's never satisfied, and that ain't a bad thing. She won't settle for less, and is always pushing for bigger and better things. Even when she was little, she could just look at something and announce, "I can do that! I can make that!" And she could. She doesn't know the word "no." She also has such a strong sense of character, and she's aware that she has a platform she can use for good. She feels her responsibility in a very powerful way. But while she's doing all this, I also have to remind her that she's eighteen, and she's got the whole world ahead of her. She doesn't have to build Rome in a day! I say take time to have fun, to count your blessings, to be in the moment, right? But in the same breath, don't let your dreams slip away. She's always getting that speech from me: "Don't be lazy; do what you set out to do and follow through. And while you're at it, clean up after yourself!" Most of the time I don't have to say it more than once because she pushes herself hard and she knows what she's doing.

In the beginning, Avani was just in her room and we never saw what she was putting together until it was posted. I was amazed by how great it was, but it was nothing special to her—she's so humble. Once, she did a video where she popped up dressed like a guy with a mustache and a flannel shirt. It still cracks me up, and I think I've watched it fifty times over.

My daughter, she's funny! She lights up when she's on camera. She's also incredibly smart. I remember thinking when all this started to blow up, she's like one of the top quarterbacks of TikTok and social media. She was figuring out which way to go, calling the shots, studying the other players. I can just hear her now: "Dad, football again, seriously?" Well, you know your social media and I know my sports. After a while, I learned to trust her instincts because she is rarely wrong. I will just say one more thing: when you see that goal line out in front of you, Voni, keep your pace steady and your wits about you. You're comin' up the right way and you will score; I know it in my bones. You've already got the one-name thing goin' on, so you might just be a JLo or a Madonna one day, and I'd be cool with that. Whatever you choose, whatever you set your sights on, know your dad is here and I gotcha.

chapter two

Throwback

©2002

*I*f you ask my parents what I was like as a little kid, they will both come up with the same word and probably put an exclamation point after it: stubborn! It's an accurate description of little me (and maybe even here-and-now me). When I was three, my parents put my older sister and me in a Taekwondo class. The instructor tried to get all the kids to respond to him "Yes, sir!" but I wouldn't do it. He got down on one knee, right in front of my face, and tried to look fierce and intimidating. I stared right back at him and kept my mouth shut. Finally, he called over a female instructor, thinking maybe she could teach me some discipline, but I just shook my head emphatically. Needless to say, my parents took me out of that class pretty quickly—and they knew they had one tough cookie on their hands.

As a kid, I rarely had tantrums, but when I did, they were *baaaaad.* Lots of screaming, kicking, crying, and throwing stuff. They went on for hours until I wore myself out. You just couldn't tell me "no" or "stop"—it was my way or the highway. So it's fitting that a road trip was the scene of one of my worst meltdowns. My family was headed to a picnic about a thirty-minute drive from our home. As my parents were unloading my stroller and food from our van, I decided to climb out myself—and I fell. I barely even scraped my knee, but I worked myself into a hysterical fit. I'm not sure if it was the pain, the sight of blood, or the fact that I had failed to demonstrate my "big girlness," but I cried and cried, screaming for a Band-Aid. My mom frantically searched the diaper bag, but there were none left. As soon as I heard that, I threw myself down and pounded the ground with my fists.

We ended up having to pack everything back up and head home. I kept it up the entire ride, climbing out of my car seat and refusing to sit still or settle. My mom had to hold me down until we got home to keep me from climbing out a window. I was so mad, I bit her arm and left huge teeth marks and a bruise. What did we learn from this episode of *Life with Avani*? Watch out . . . I bite! I could be quite the tiny terror when the mood struck.

Before the terrible toddler years, my mom says I was a lovely little baby. Calm, content, a good sleeper, and very, very quiet. I was born November 23, 2002, in Indianapolis, Indiana. I'm told I was my mom's easiest pregnancy and delivery, and I even came a couple days early. I guess I was eager to make my grand entrance in the world. My parents were super stressed because Shanti's delivery was a nightmare, so they were anticipating mine would be the same. Lucky for them, I cooperated. Mom gave a few good pushes and out I came. Shanti was very excited to have a new baby sister or brother—my parents didn't want to know my gender until I arrived on the scene. Surprise! It's a girl . . . again! In keeping with my mom's heritage, my parents gave me a traditional Indian name. Avani means "earth," and my family calls me "Voni" for short.

As a baby, I mostly wore onesies, but as soon as I was old enough to dress myself, I would change my outfits at least two to three times during the day. I didn't like anything girly or fancy; I wanted to run around in sweatshirts, tee shirts, and tights. Such a fashionista. If I'm being perfectly honest, I still switch it up all day. I have always loved fashion and styling myself. Also, I can never decide what I want to wear, so I wear it all!

As a kid, I was a very active tomboy who would tumble, stand on my head, and do gymnastics all over the house. You could not convince me that a couch was made for sitting—it was my private indoor trampoline. The specific deets may be fuzzy, but I remember having a whole lotta energy and needing to let it out. Gymnastics was a great outlet (more on that later). At the same time, I could be a quiet loner with a big imagination. I liked to draw and color, make all kinds of craft projects, and just be in my own little world. I was a middle kid, but I never fought with my sisters over toys or games—they could keep 'em. I was never very attached to dolls, stuffed animals, or any of the things girls my age begged for. However, I do remember watching *Dora* and *Blue's Clues* and being slightly obsessed with *The Wiggles*—they were my very first concert. They danced around with a big dinosaur and a pirate. Today, it would probably give me nightmares, but at the time, I was extremely into it. Do not hold it against me.

Our home was a ranch-style house with three bedrooms, a huge backyard, and a swing set. Once I was out of the crib, Shanti and I shared a bedroom. Our neighborhood was surrounded by stores and a movie theater. When we were older, we would ride our bikes over to the video store to rent movies. Shanti's first gymnastics gym was just down the street. Basically,

I wanted to do whatever she did, so I started imitating any moves she was learning. One day, my parents were watching Shanti flip around the living room and, out of nowhere, I did one perfectly clean, one-handed cartwheel after another. No one had ever taught me; it just came naturally. My parents stared in disbelief. "In that moment, we realized you had a gift," my dad explains, "and we knew we had to help you explore it."

That week, they took me to Dana Mannix Gymnastics in Indianapolis, where they had all these little tumble mats, rope ladders, and trampolines—all the basic stuff. I had fun, but it was way too easy. After just one session, the instructor came over and said, "You need to take her to DeVeau's School of Gymnastics." I think my mom and dad were a little shocked. DeVeau's was a hard-core, high-competition gym that had trained several girls for the Olympics. But I was ready and willing to show them what I could do. Tumbling was baby stuff; I wanted to fly.

We needed to have an appointment at DeVeau's for me to even try out, and there was a waiting list. But, finally, they told me to come in. My parents sat on the sidelines, not expecting much. I was four years old, had never trained before, and this all seemed out of my league. "Voni, don't be afraid when you go out there," my dad said. "Do the best that you can and have fun!" I guess after going through all the tests, I wowed them. Coach Kim came over: "She's amazing. She's on the team." Just like that, my gymnastics journey began.

At first, I went to practice for an hour a day, then two to three hours, and eventually four hours. Once I got into the higher levels, I spent twenty-two hours a week at the gym Monday through Saturday. In third grade, we moved into a larger, two-story house with a full basement, four bedrooms, plus a huge bonus room. At first, I plastered my room with One Direction posters, followed by pics of Twenty One Pilots. As I began to accumulate gymnastics trophies, we put them on display. I had too many medals to count, so those all got boxed up for safekeeping.

DeVeau's was about an hour away from our new home, depending on traffic. It didn't seem like a burden at the time—at least not to me, but I wasn't the one driving! My practice just became part of our daily routine as a family, and we worked around it. As I made my way up the levels, there was always something new to master: an extra twist, a flip, or a new move. Then it had to be cleaned and sharpened. I loved it, but I was also never satisfied. Maybe that's what kept me pushing on— the need to do better and be the best.

Yes, the coaches were demanding and expected us to pull our weight as a team, but a lot of my competitive drive came from within. I had a personal best that I demanded of myself in every skill. The only thing I hated was beam, probably because it's all about balance, which is not something I naturally possess. I'm not really into taking cautious steps, one foot in front of the other. Beam also requires walking a straight, narrow line, which is something that goes against every fiber of my being. But my coaches refused to let me check out: "If you fall in a competition, you're going to have to get up and finish or you're just going to look dumb in front of everyone." Way to instill confidence in a kid, right? I would always get hurt on beam, but I would also always get back up and keep going. I didn't realize it at the time, but it was teaching me an important life lesson about resilience, which would come in handy when I had to switch gears in my career down the line. Isn't it funny how the stuff we go through when we're young gives us the tools we need to deal with life's ups and downs when we're older? Good thing I paid attention.

Still, I was never a big fan of school—many people don't know this about me, but I was in high honors classes (yes, I took AP classes, too). Those of you who are in honors classes know the extra stress and pressure that it can bring into your normal, everyday life. Not only that, I also have a tough time sitting for long periods of time (like, anything longer than ten minutes, unless it's a really, really good movie!) and listening to someone go on and on about a subject. I think my best "education" came from my experiences in the gym. That's where I learned the most about myself and what I am capable of if I let go of fear. Basically, there's no room for being afraid in gymnastics. You either go for it or you go home. Little kids especially have no fear. Watch a five-year-old learn to do a backflip and you'll see what I mean. They throw themselves into it because they have no reason to believe they can't execute it perfectly. They take death-defying leaps without hesitation and tackle life without any limits. When you're older, you lose that spirit and start to ask "Why?" instead of "Why not?" I used to be fearless. I remember it well, but somewhere along the way, I lost it. I guess life just got real, and little kids make their own reality.

The more time I spent at the gym, the harder it was for me to just be a normal kid. No one at my school really understood why I always had to miss parties or playdates; they didn't get why I wanted to spend every waking minute training. Family and friends questioned if my parents were pushing me too much and if all this was "good for me." Let's be clear: I was the one pushing. The gymnastics season started in October when the weather began to get cooler, which meant it conflicted with school. I begged my parents to let me enroll in online classes so I could focus on what I loved, but they worried I was putting all my eggs in one basket. What if I suddenly decided gymnastics wasn't fun anymore? I couldn't just give up on school; I had to have a backup plan. Before I started online schooling, I stuck it out as long as I could, which meant constantly fighting with my teachers. They wanted me to take gym class, which my parents thought was ridiculous since I was getting plenty of exercise. And we pleaded with my teachers not to penalize me for missing so many days to attend practice and meets. However, according to my school, gymnastics was a "hobby," an extracurricular that shouldn't interfere with my education.

I didn't care what people thought. I loved hitting the road for meets. There were times when we would have to leave our home at four a.m. to drive to a competition that was four hours away. When it was over in the early evening, we'd turn around and drive back home, and I would get up for school the next day, barely able to keep my eyes open in class. Other times, we would fly to a big away meet with teams from other states and districts. That was the best because it involved staying in a hotel and "escaping" my day-to-day life. One of my favorite things was when I reached level 7 and I got to choose my own music for my floor routine. I was very dedicated to mixing mine. My mom and I worked hard on finding something unique because I wanted to be different. I didn't want to have the same music as anyone else. When my music came on, it was stuff that no one had heard before. It had to be instrumental, so I would find slow and fast pieces and mix them together to form a whole new sound. It may have confused some of the audience and more than a few judges. I loved commanding their attention. I admire Olympic gymnasts like Laurie Hernandez and Gabby Douglas, and American Cup winner Katelyn Ohashi. I am in awe of not just their athleticism, but their artistry. They were each so unique in how they embraced the sport. Fun fact: a few years down the road, Katelyn actually DM'd me to say she was fan of mine on TikTok! I was like, "You are a fan of *me*? You're a collegiate world record holder! I am shook!"

Seeing how other young gymnasts were shaking things up also empowered me. Besides changing the soundtrack, I wanted to stand out with my style. I never did basic hair, either: I'd put in a bunch of colorful rubber bands and spray glitter all over my head. I guess I've always pushed the boundaries. After all, the thing I hate most is being boring. In the world of gymnastics, that can work for you or against you. Sometimes I got hated on for my uniqueness—gymnasts, moms, and coaches just didn't understand me. But I would never worry what people thought about me. If they're talking about you, you're doing something right.

I have been marching to my own beat since the day I was old enough to take my first steps. Maybe if I had tried harder to fit in, I would have had it easier, but if you haven't figured it out by now, I don't do "easy." If something is difficult or if someone says it can't be done, it's Code Avani for "Just do it." That kind of determination can get you far, but it can also get you in trouble. For the longest time I thought I was unstoppable. I thought nothing could break me or shake me. But the fact is, you can't stay a little kid forever. At some point in your life, you have to accept your weaknesses and admit you're vulnerable. Even Superman's got his kryptonite, right? In my case, my weaknesses were both physical and mental, and I stubbornly refused to let them stop me—until they did just that.

Run It Back: Is Stubbornness a Good Thing?

Stubbornness doesn't have the best rep, especially when you're a woman, but it *can* serve you well. I'm not telling you to tune out everyone's opinion but your own—no one can be right 100 percent of the time. But I have found plenty of instances where being strong-headed worked for me. When, you ask? Let me spell it out for you:

+ When you need to make a decision. Sticking to your guns gives you an edge. It allows you to trust your gut. When others might waver, you know where you stand.

+ When someone is trying to steal your thunder, especially in competition. In gymnastics, I stubbornly refused to lose. Winners are often stubborn because they won't give in or give up until they get what they want.

+ When someone asks you to settle. I am never satisfied with second best. If your stubbornness propels you to get better results—to want better

things for yourself and the world in general—
I say go for it.

✦ When the crowd says, "Follow us." Stubborn
peeps can resist mob mentality. They possess
inner strength to combat being pushed. Instead,
they push back . . . hard.

✦ When something isn't working. Stubborn people
will ask, "Is there a better way to approach this?"
They question how something is done, maybe
because it's not how they would do it. Yeah, it
may be a little self-indulgent, but it can also lead
to exciting and creative solutions. All those guys
who invented stuff like light bulbs, the internet,
and Frappuccinos? I'm sure they were stubborn
as mules. I owe ya.

On Avani

My big sis, Shanti Gregg, says:

Avani is beautiful inside and out. She is known for putting others first, and she has been that way since a young age. She takes care of her family and her friends 24/7. She is outgoing, strong, and ambitious, and strives to be better every single day.

We both love to be on social media and go out together. Our younger sister, Priya, doesn't really care for either, so whenever I want to go somewhere or take pictures, Avani is my go-to girl. We both really love to shop, as well. Avani tends to be shy off social media, but she can also be strongheaded and very funny. There is a lot I love about Avani, but my favorite thing is her personality. She makes everyone in the room laugh, and that's when I know she is being her true self. Avani has always made my sad days into happy ones. That said, the one thing that absolutely drives me crazy is that she can't take someone re-peating a question. I will ask her if she wants food. She will say yes but not give me any specifics. I will ask her what she wants, and she will get mad: "Why are you asking me another question?!" It's pretty hilarious, and of course I have to keep asking just to irritate her more.

Voni has always been unique and special in my eyes. She has incredible talent when it comes to makeup. She has been doing it since she was in middle school and she has always been passionate about it. I remember her coming home after four-hour gymnastics practices and doing full makeup looks on school nights just to make a few Musical.lys. She has so much self-determined drive, and I admire it. In high school, even when Avani was focused on school and gymnastics, the one thing you could always rely on was Avani making content every single day, no matter how hard it was.

Of course, this didn't completely rule out time for going to concerts. I remember when we went to see Harry Styles, I was wearing a black crop top with high-waisted black jeans. We had another spectator take our picture together. When we looked at the shot, we saw that the whole side of my stomach was out of my jeans. We literally cry-laughed about it for at least twenty minutes. To this very day I can show her that picture when she's having a rough day and it will make her crack up.

Avani is also beyond generous. I can't even count all the nice things she's done for me. She bought me my *dream purse and took me as her plus-one to Milan. We sat in the front row for the Dolce & Gabbana fashion show, and our entire time in Italy felt like a fever dream because it was so magical. She could have taken anyone else, but Avani chose me because she knew I love fashion and traveling.*

The past two years have been life-changing for Avani. She has been doing so many big things, and I am incredibly proud of her. There will always be highs and lows when it comes to social media; I've seen Avani thriving and I've seen her in super-depressive states. No one would have ever thought we would be put into this situation, but she's living her best life and doing what she loves. That is a blessing not just to her, but to our entire family.

chapter three

Did a Full 180

*G*rowing up, it was always my dream to one day go to the Olympics. I'd been taking gymnastics classes and competing in this sport since I was four years old. This was my ultimate end goal. I was going to stand on that podium, wave to the crowd, and accept my gold medal for the U.S. It was more than a dream; I could see it so clearly. I also imagined myself being recruited by a top collegiate team and making my mark there. Maybe UCLA, where Katelyn Ohashi had competed? That had a nice ring to it. I had plans, big plans, bruh! I was sixteen, a training level 10 gymnast, and well on my way to achieving everything I wanted. But that's exactly when life sneaks up on you and says, "Oh yeah? Think again." That's what happened to me in 2018, and for a while I was in total denial. It's probably the reason why I kept going, injuring myself more and more, to the point where I could no longer compete. When that happened, it was like the walls came crashing down around me. Without gymnastics, I didn't know who I was, much less who I could be.

It started with a stress fracture in my back. As a gymnast, I was used to bumps, bruises, sprains, and achy joints, but this pain was something I had never felt before. It was sharp, piercing, and persistent. I couldn't stand up completely straight without having tears roll down my face. It took months for me to accept that it was much worse than we thought—it was career ending. But it took a long time for me to even slow down. My broken back has its own backstory. What you should know is that I gave it all I had. I gave it a fight to the finish. I'm not sure if that helped or hurt the situation. I only know how it ended—not well.

Since I promised to be 100 percent honest with you in this book, let me confess that writing about this wasn't as easy as I thought it would be. I figured I would be over it by now and it would feel like some distant memory. But when I actually sat down to revisit the experience, and I had to play back all those details in my head, I realized my back may not hurt anymore but my heart does. It's all still a little raw. I hope that will eventually fade with time, but I'm going to lay it all out for you now.

In 2011, we moved so my parents could be closer to their families. We had been living in Fishers because Dad was in the fire department there, and when he resigned, there was really no reason to stay in that area. Because of the move, I had to leave my former gym, DeVeau's School of Gymnastics, and start up at a new gym. I didn't stay at this new place for very long; let's just say that their training regimen wasn't for me. One day, while heading to practice, I told my dad I didn't want to do gymnastics anymore if I had to stay there. So he made *me* go inside and tell the head coach that I was quitting. My parents would never let my sisters and me start something and not see it to the end.

After I quit gymnastics, my parents insisted I find another

sport, so I joined the local soccer team. I made it through one season and I enjoyed it, but it wasn't competitive enough for me. Only a handful of kids took it seriously at that beginning age. After that, I had some time off, but not for long. I really missed gymnastics and wanted to go back, so my parents found Sharp's Gymnastics Academy in Indianapolis. Sharp's became not only my gym, but also my second home. In August 2015, I got called into the guidance counselor's office during class. "Avani, I have some bad news . . ." The guidance counselor told me that the owner and head coach at Sharp's had been arrested for four counts of child molestation and three counts of sexual misconduct with a minor. My mom had called the school and asked the guidance counselor to tell me the breaking news before another student did. I was stunned and crying so hard I had to go home. Thank God nothing had happened to me at Sharp's, but I felt so bad for the person who had come forward. I also knew what it meant: my mom pulled me out of Sharp's that very day and enrolled me at Interactive Academy in Zionsville, thirty minutes away from home.

Starting at the new gym was hard; it meant getting to know new coaches and teammates. I guess all that stress distracted me and I injured my toe while practicing on the beam. In the world of athletic injuries, an injured toe is no biggie, but once it healed, I sprained my ankle while vaulting. Then I injured one of my core stomach muscles while practicing my floor routine. That one took me out of practice for a good couple of weeks. When it healed, I got a hairline fracture in both of my knees while doing vault. The tendon that goes from my knee to the tibia had been pulled so hard that it fractured the bone. On top of that, an old hip injury also flared up, which triggered my back. You see a pattern here? I was falling apart! The intense training was heating me up and I had to go to physical therapy all the time. Can you imagine the medical bills my parents were paying?

Because of my hip injury, my pelvis was off-center, so I would get recurring injuries near my hip and lumbar area. But eventually, after my hip healed, I went right back to doing full practice, which is when I felt this strange, sharp, constant pain in my lower back. I didn't think too much of it. I'd had so many injuries that I'd conditioned myself to simply push through the pain. There was no reason for me to think this was any different, or any more serious. But then it became a constant gnawing ache, and it continued to intensify. My coaches saw how much pain I was in and insisted I see a doctor. My parents were worried because I could barely stand up straight anymore, and they were afraid I was doing permanent damage to my body. So I had an MRI and was told my back was "slightly fractured, not to worry, it will heal pretty quickly." I wore a back brace to sleep and tried not to cry at night when throbbing pain from lying on the hard plastic shell of the brace kept me awake. Plus, I was not able to move around or stretch. It felt like I was in a straitjacket, but I had to wear it 24/7, only taking it off to shower. I had physical therapy once a week and exercises to do three times a day. Heating or icing it didn't help, but I kept telling myself it was just a temporary setback and kept on training. I didn't want to lose my momentum.

I ignored the signs and didn't listen to my body telling me it was too much. Then, one day, I was doing floor and could no longer complete my leap pass, which is when you jump up in the air, do the splits, and land with your feet together. This was one of my favorite skills to perform, but getting my legs out and off the ground at the same time was impossible. I felt intense pain in my lower back, right where the fracture was. Eventually, I had to sit out practices and meets because it was too excruciating. It was also pretty obvious to everyone, including me, that my range of motion was becoming limited. I went to competitions to support my teammates, but while I cheered them on, I saw my dreams slipping away.

The gym was willing to let me keep training at a slower pace. I thought that if an elite or Olympic career was out of the question, at least I could compete on the bars at a college level. I didn't have to do all the events; I could just do what my body could handle. But that plan fell apart pretty quickly too. After about three months, my doctor—a sports medicine specialist—had to sit me down and deliver the bad news I knew was coming: it was over. My back would never recover enough for me to compete again. The only way it could completely heal—and not permanently impact my health—was if I stopped gymnastics, did my physical therapy, and waited it out for six months or more. It wasn't just, "Take a little break and then you can go back." I knew I would lose most of my high-level skills and I would have to start all over. I was getting too close to graduation and was afraid I wouldn't have the skills I needed to get a college scholarship. So it was time to hang it up.

I remember hearing the words my doctor said, but not completely processing them. I started to cry while I was in her office, and I could tell my mom was tearing up, too. I was feeling so many emotions, but all I could latch on to was numbness. More than denial, I was in shock. Gymnastics had been so much more than a sport for me. It was where I could release my anger and frustration; it was truly my outlet and my therapy. If I couldn't do it anymore, I would be completely lost. Adding to this agony was the fact that I also felt guilty for all the time and money my family had poured into my training—what a waste! What about my coaches who had worked so hard to prepare me? My teammates who counted on me? I couldn't bear the thought of letting everyone down. How could I ever face them? What would I say? "Sorry I ruined everything, but hey, it was great while it lasted"?

My mom said I had to go through the stages of grief and mourn the loss of gymnastics before I could move on. Denial, anger, bargaining, depression, and finally, acceptance. It was frighteningly accurate. I spent time in each stage—first in a trance, then furious at everything and everyone. Next, I tried rationalizing, "This isn't so bad . . . is it?" and tried to convince myself that everything was going to be okay. Then came the giant wave of what I can only describe as wallowing. I just wanted to be left alone to feel very, very bad for myself. Self-pity and "woe is me" wrapped up into one giant ball of sadness. Wow, I was a mess. It makes sense to me now, but at the time, it was like someone had pressed the pause button on my life. What I remember most is bawling my eyes out—and we all know puffy raccoon eyes are not pretty on anyone.

My family tried to comfort me, even though it was very hard for them as well. For twelve years, they lived gymnastics with me. To this day, they can't watch an old gymnastics video of me without crying. Regardless of how much they tried to comfort me, I was devastated. Dad likes to compare everything to football: "Think of Peyton Manning or Brett Favre, all those greats who had to hang up their shoulder pads. They transitioned, as hard as it was." All I kept hearing from everyone around me was, "You're sixteen. You have your whole life ahead of you." But it didn't feel that way. It felt like my life was over, and I wanted to scream, "Please don't try and tell me it's not, you don't know what I'm going through!" Loss is very personal. It's different for everyone, and it doesn't come with a set schedule. You're gonna feel what you're gonna feel when you feel it. No deadlines, no way to keep it neat and tidy or tuck it away for a while. Grief will stick around as long as it needs to, as long as you let it.

It was my mom's little tough love lecture that finally got through to me. She came into my room and sat down beside me. I was in my usual spot in bed with the covers pulled over my head. I curled myself up in a ball even tighter. I knew what was coming.

"Voni, we've got to try and rethink this now, right? What you thought was going to be your life is not that anymore."

I shook my head. Not helping, Mom. Go away.

"You can sit here and mope or find something new to do," she continued. "Your decision."

My decision? Was she kidding? It wasn't my decision to kiss my career goodbye; the doctors and coaches and *you guys* made it for me. It also wasn't my decision to feel this miserable, it was the only way I knew how to react to the worst thing that had ever happened to me.

"It's time to get over it."

Get over it? That would mean getting up, and I was determined not to budge from my bed. Avani's not here, leave a message! That's when Mom pulled the covers off. That was her not-so-subtle way of telling me that enough was enough. I couldn't go on like this. I had to find something that made me happy again, something to fill the void. Ugh.

Of course, Mom being Mom, she was full of suggestions, since I couldn't see them through all my angst. Her best advice?

Makeup and acting had always been a fun sideline, but now they could be front and center if I made the effort to get off my butt. Luckily for me, when I was forced to rest out all my injuries, I would stay up late, do my makeup, and post on Musical.ly, before it became TikTok. I enjoyed expressing myself through makeup and acting, but I never once saw it as a possible career. My mom insisted there was more to me than just gymnastics. On some level, I knew that was true. But it required me to rethink everything I had hung my hopes on. It required me to switch gears. I had always been so strong, but right now, all I felt was shattered. "You can pick up the pieces," Mom said, patting me on the back. "I believe in you." Maybe I just needed to hear it so I could believe in myself. Maybe I *could* be me again—just Me 2.0.

I know it might sound a bit dramatic, but social media saved me. It gave me a plan B. It also taught me how to bounce back. Here's the thing: you discover who you really are and what you're made of when you're face-to-face with uncertainty. Loss sucks. I'm not going to sugarcoat it. Having the rug pulled out from under you is *the worst*, but you can stand up and find your balance again. That goes for careers, relationships, college admissions, and more. The pain might feel so intense that you can't imagine ever getting past it. But you will. You will survive, I pinky swear. It takes a little faith and imagination to see the excitement and possibility in the unknown. Can you trust the universe just a little bit and see where it takes you?

If you're shaking your head no, I totally get it. If you had told me I would one day find something that made me feel happier and more fulfilled than gymnastics, I would have called you crazy. Gymnastics was my do or die. But now, I see that I had to go through that tremendous loss to come out on the other side. I'm gonna be straight with you: life isn't fair. Things don't always work out the way you plan, and you can't always get what you want. Disappointment is kind of inevitable. One day, you're going to be blindsided and pissed beyond belief that what you thought was a given is gone, gone, gone and it's not coming back. But think about it: loss isn't what defines us, it's the way we handle it that counts. That's one of Dad's oldie-but-goodie pieces of advice (I told you, sometimes they stick!). So yeah, I had to train my brain to bounce back, and it was a serious workout. I had to struggle and stretch to see the possibilities. But guess what? I'm a stronger person because of it. I'm more willing to take risks and more open to new opportunities that might come my way because I've seen that I'm capable of change. Maybe I deserve a gold medal for that?

During the pandemic, so many people talked about needing to "pivot" because life didn't look the same anymore. We didn't have a choice. We had to go about our lives in a strange new way and be cool with masks, social distancing, and Zoom classes. Like Dua Lipa says, sometimes you gotta do "a full 180." TBH, I used to get queasy on those thrill rides at amusement parks. But 180s don't scare me or even make me dizzy anymore. In fact, I kind of welcome the chance to challenge myself. Sometimes you grow when you let it go. To this day, I still say I'm a gymnast. I'll be a gymnast forever. I just added a few more lines to my bio, so I'm that much more fabulous.

I may have suffered a loss, but I gained so much. I found a new tribe in social media circles. I found my beb. I found new interests and so many things that make me excited to wake up in the morning and kick off those covers (don't worry, Mom, I'll make my bed!). Do I occasionally feel a pang of longing for my old life? Sure. But the more time passes, the less I miss it. I may never entirely "get over" something that was my everything, but that's okay. I won't let that loss stand in the way of new dreams. And that's the point, isn't it? You're capable of so much more than you could ever imagine. I firmly believe that everything happens for a reason. If I was still competing in gymnastics, I would not have moved to LA; met any of my friends; won a Shorty Award; graced the cover of *Seventeen*; gotten brand sponsorships with Doritos, Fila, L'Oréal, Morphe, and Louis Vuitton; played Gemma on Brat TV's *Chicken Girls*; been chosen for *Forbes* 30 Under 30; or had my own show, *Here For It with Avani Gregg* on Messenger Watch Together. You get the point. If I was still in gymnastics, I would have missed out on all these amazing opportunities to build my "empire," as my dad put it. Hey, I wouldn't even be writing this book or getting to connect with you! I can't believe how things have changed so radically in such a short period of time. My transformation didn't start off easy. I was determined to hold on to the grief. But because of my loss, I gained more than I ever thought possible.

Losing something or someone you love with all your heart is so, so hard, but it makes you stronger. Maybe you're in a place where you can't or won't see that right now, and that's perfectly fine. Take the time you need to be in your feels and sort things through. Wallow away like I did because it's your right. But one day, I promise you'll look back at what I wrote here and be like, "Damn! Avani called it!" I told you so. I've been there, done that, and I guarantee I will do it again. But I hope I won't be such a wreck next time something or someone blindsides me. Because now I know that doing a 180 is all part of growing up, finding your way, and figuring out your passion and purpose. For me, it was a major breakthrough just putting these words down on the page and seeing the progress I've made. My back might not have healed the way it was supposed to, but my heart is definitely getting there.

Run It Back: How to Bounce

I used to love jumping on a trampoline in the gym—that feeling of falling and immediately bouncing right back into the air, higher and higher each time. I wish it was that easy to rebound from loss, failure, or disappointment, but practice makes perfect.

✦ Think positive. Making your brain go to a happy place when you're down is tough, but optimism can help you see things more clearly. My mom laid it all out for me and helped me take stock of everything I had going for me. She reminded me of what I loved, what I was good at, and how bright my future was. Hope heals, just sayin'.

✦ Expect the unexpected. That way, when it shows up on your doorstep, you're not totally overwhelmed and unable to cope. The world is full of change, especially these days, so it can't hurt to mentally prepare yourself to pivot.

✦ You've got the power. By this, I mean you can choose what comes next. You can sit in bed bawling your eyes out or you can decide to move forward, make plans, and morph into a new person capable of greatness. I'd go with that . . .

✦ Ask for help, especially if you're feeling as sad and adrift as I was. There is no shame or blame if you can't dig your way out by yourself. Loss will knock you on your butt. Reach out to people who love you for support, advice, and cheerleading. Lean on them until you feel strong enough to stand on your own two feet.

✦ Say thank you. I mean it. Be grateful and appreciative of everything you have in your daily life. One loss, even if it's a biggie, does not negate all the good stuff. Gratitude helps you keep things in perspective. Vacation plans canceled? They forgot the sauce for your chicken nuggets? Don't freak the freak out; you've got so much going for you.

On Avani

My gymnastics coach Eric Philabaum says:

> I first met Avani in August 2015, when she was thirteen or fourteen. It was clear that she was very talented and an extremely hard worker. She would make things look effortless because she wouldn't be satisfied until they did. She was a great teammate—always encouraging, always cheering for everyone. She was a great example to younger kids at the gym and showed them how to approach gymnastics: with hard work and perseverance. Make it look good, put your own spin on it to stand out, and make the judges notice you. I coached Avani on bars and vault, where her strongest skills were her bail to handstand and toe shoot catch on the high bar. A bail is a skill that the gymnast does to transition from the high bar to the low. What Avani could do was do a handstand on the low bar, grab the low bar with her toes, and then swing around, shoot up, and grab onto the high bar. She was always pushing the envelope and she had flair in everything she did, which made her the center of attention even though she wasn't trying to be. She has a kind heart and a great personality. Her teammates just loved being around her.

It was devastating when Avani had to quit. You could see the fire leaving her eyes. It was heartbreaking when she told her coaches and teammates that she had to be done. I give credit to her family and her friends for helping her through it. Social media and schoolwork helped Avani keep busy. But I understand that she still misses gymnastics. Once a gymnast, always a gymnast.

chapter four

Clown Girl

A lot of interviewers ask me how I got into "all this," meaning social media. Most kids fool around on the apps and don't take it too seriously. I didn't either at first. I was twelve and just goofing around on Musical.ly. Funny story (isn't there always?): I would be nowhere in social media without sign language. When I was in seventh grade, I became interested in American Sign Language (ASL). I thought it was so cool to be able to communicate without using your voice, so I marched into the guidance office and requested to take sign language instead of Spanish. Just one small problem: ASL wasn't offered at my school. *Fine*, I thought, *be that way. I'll figure it out on my own.* I threw myself into it, following and duetting all kinds of ASL creators on the app. Eventually I transferred to online schooling and found out that ASL was being offered as an online class. Well, you guessed it: Sign me up, please! I loved being able to communicate with the deaf community. At first, I had maybe two hundred followers, and I would do these Boomerang videos: "That's the sign of the day, everyone!" Then I saw an ASL TikTok challenge and decided to give it a shot. I signed to a song that was trending, and guess what? I won! The prize was a duet with one of the ASL creators. That was the first time I felt "known."

I had been on the app for six years and I found all the little trends that were going, adding my own twists to them. I was pretty analytical about it: I would research what was popular, then ask myself, "What have I not shown that people would like?" I posted my artwork, gymnastics skills, and funny videos. I was going live a lot, too, so I could talk to followers and ask them how they were doing. I wanted them to know I was real and they could trust me. I guess I was doing something right, because my videos started blowing up.

The crazy makeup looks came later, but they were also self-taught. Some people wear their heart on their sleeve. Me? I wear mine on my face. Every emotion, everything I'm wrestling with or stressing about, I express it through my makeup. It's always been my art. When I was eleven, I would spend every cent of my allowance on eyeshadow palettes, brushes, lipsticks, and liners. At the time, I was just playing around; I loved drawing, and this was a way to throw my artwork from paper to my face. It was basically the same—lines and colors, shading and blending. The only difference? It was *alive*. And in drawing and painting on myself, art became a lot more personal. It became who I am, not just what I did. It became an extension of my inner self.

Makeup is a great outlet for me—I highly recommend it. My mom showed me the basics and I watched a few people on YouTube, but then I figured things out on my own. I was not educated in face paint or special FX makeup. I just threw lines on my face and experimented. Some things worked, some didn't, but I grew very comfortable just picking up a brush and going to town on my face. I would never copy exactly what another makeup artist did. I feel like that's disrespecting their art. So when fans started copying my work, I got really upset. "Are they making fun of me?" Truly, that's where my mind always goes when my insecurity kicks in. Each of my looks had a very personal meaning, so I worried that when fans knocked them off, they were taking a direct hit at me. It made me doubt if I wanted to post anymore. "Voni, imitation is the sincerest form of flattery." That's another wise ol' saying my parents like to bat at me. Eventually, I learned to see that I was inspiring people, and that felt a whole lot better than assuming I was the butt of their jokes.

Clown Girl was actually born out of a dare. It was June 2019, and I was hanging out with a friend, scrolling through videos, when I found the "Clown Check!" audio edit of "Hokus Pokus" by Insane Clown Posse. "That's cool," I said, and the wheels started turning. It wasn't the first time I had done clown makeup on myself, and I could see how this sound might work for me. I feel that the sound often inspires the makeup—it triggers an idea that I can springboard off of.

"Ew," my friend groaned. "I hate that TikTok trend. It's creepy. Don't do it."

She should have known better. Now I had to prove her wrong. Not only could the sound work, but I could do a makeup look based upon it and see how people would react to it. I knew I wanted to make the transition from my own face to clown face very dramatic, so I painted red and blue stars over my eyes and put in white contacts so my pupils disappeared. I painted on a twisted red mouth, a red nose, and a blue tongue. I looked kind of possessed, which was the idea. Sinister, demonic, crazeeee! The whole video is maybe fifteen seconds long, and it goes from me in no makeup and natural daylight to a clown girl shadowed in purple and laughing her head off as she sings, "Abracadabra boom shacka dae! I'm Violent J, and I'm back like a vertebrae!"

I went to bed and woke up to 2 million views! Yup, completely insane. I remember thinking, *What is going on here? Is someone punking me?* A lot of people thought I based the look on Harley Quinn, but I hadn't seen the movie yet and I had no idea who the character was. They also thought that the audio was my voice, but it's actually another girl. She got pissed at me for stealing the Clown Check crown away from her, but I can't undo it. From that moment on, my life has never been the same. People started coming up to me all the time, recognizing me on the street. I had to quit my job as a lifeguard because I would get noticed at work and people would ask to take pictures with me. It eventually got really weird. No one even knew my name, they just called me "Clown Girl," as in, "Hey, Clown Girl, can we make a TikTok?" or "Hey, Clown Girl, how's it going?" My mom shook her head. "Who is this Clown Girl? Do we have to change your name to Clown Girl Gregg?" She was teasing, but it did feel like I was no longer me. It was strange and scary, but also pretty sick.

About a month later, things really began to take off. I was flying back and forth between Indiana and LA to meet brands and go to events, and my manager would let me stay in her guesthouse. It was a six-hour flight, but I had serious FOMO and never wanted to miss an opportunity. At first, my mom was cool with me being on the West Coast by myself, but then she started worrying (what moms do best). "You cannot be in LA by yourself anymore. You're only sixteen and your father and I don't like it." She found a way to work remotely, and we moved into a one-bedroom apartment in LA while my dad and sisters stayed in Indiana. I know my parents thought this was a good solution, but it was hard on Mom because she was separated from her husband and kids while I was out filming and making content.

"I think if we do this, we should do it as a family," she told me. "All of us." So, seven months later, my dad sold our house in Indiana and moved to LA with Priya. All four of us (plus two dogs) lived in that one-bedroom apartment for a month and a half. It was a little cramped and crowded, but we were all finally together, where we belonged. Luckily, we ended up finding a five-bedroom house to rent while we searched for a home to buy.

I don't think there was ever a moment where I said to myself, "Okay, I'm famous now." It's ironic that when I was designing the Clown Girl video makeup, I wanted my clown to be the star of the show. That's where the stars around her eyes came into play. I didn't realize it would also turn me into the star of my own show. By now, I can't even tell you how many clown looks I've done—hundreds, not counting the ones I haven't filmed that are waiting in my sketchbook. My makeup posts took on a life of their own as I began to add backstories to each video. It wasn't just me playing around with different colors and special FX; it became a way for me to connect with people. Like I've said before, I can be shy and withdrawn, but when I put on makeup, I become this whole new person. The actor is unleashed!

Some people get it, and some people don't. I get a lot of comments that are really positive like, "Wow! Preach, bebe!" or "You a baddie and you know it!" and "Hiii, Queen!" Others tell me "Just take a pill and chill" or "You look mad, whassup with that?" In the beginning, I was all about the element of mystery. I just wanted people to vibe with the look and not put too much energy into the interpretation. Then it dawned on me that maybe something more could come of this. If there was a backstory to each look, why not share it? Why not open it up for discussion, validate what others are feeling, and allow us all to connect on a much deeper level? Let me give you an example: On October 6, 2019, I posted what looked like this cute little doll makeup. The caption was, "I'm just a toy to you." Now let's dig a little deeper. During that time, I was ghosted by this guy and it turned into a big social media situation. He put our private business out there and made me look like the bad guy. So this post was my reaction to that. I felt played. Get it? Toy? Play?

Another time, I posted a similar doll look, but I had my mouth taped up and cotton coming out of it. The caption was, "Your favorite candy's cotton and that's why your teeth are rotten." That's from a Melanie Martinez song (love her), and the post was based on some shoots that I did with a brand that originally told me to be myself and do what I wanted to do. Then they were throwing these words in my mouth, making me say things that I didn't want to say, things that didn't feel like me. I know that when you sign a contract with a brand, you have a professional obligation to give them what they want, but I won't stand for someone twisting my words. That's what the doll look was trying to say: you think you can speak for me, well, you can't.

Sometimes my look and my comment are opposites, and that has meaning as well. During the BLM protests last summer, I felt like there was a lot of unrest in the world and it had me sad and shook. I'm not a political person and I don't consider myself an activist, but it hit me hard, especially when people started accusing me of being "white and privileged." I'm Mongolian, Indian, African American, and zero percent white, so I don't know where they got that. I've made it perfectly clear that my family did not have a lot of money. We had what we needed, not always what we wanted. We were not fancy-pants people, sorry to disappoint. This was a very hard time for me. I was trying to figure out if I was actually depressed because I wasn't getting out of bed, I wasn't eating, and I wasn't posting. I threw this makeup face on with a really sad, frowning mouth, and posted the comment, "Happy!" My bebes picked up on it instantly: "You okay? I'm worried about you!" I wasn't looking for sympathy, I just wanted people to know, "FYI, this is what I'm *really* feeling, despite the happy faces you see on social media." It was a plea for people—me included—to be honest about their mental health. You can't be living in today's world and be happy all the time—you'd have to be pretty oblivious if you were. Judging from the thousands of comments, I struck a nerve. A lot of people were feeling the same way I was and, since I put it out there, we could all talk about it.

Anything and everything motivates me. It can be something I'm going through in the moment, or something I experienced a long time ago. It can be something I read or see on TV or socials. It can be something that makes me sad or angry or laugh out loud. I especially love sharing my take on something that is really popular. For example, everyone was posting covers of Olivia Rodrigo's song "Drivers License." It was the top trend on the TikTok Discover Page and number one on the iTunes charts. I had to go for it . . . my way. So I filmed myself sitting in my car, staring out the window, eating my chicken nuggets. Read into it what you will. A lot of fans asked if I had broken up with Anthony (as if), but the truth is I was hungry and sitting in the car when some dude walked by and I was watching him watch me. It just struck me as funny.

A lot of the time, my videos start with a sound. I am constantly looking for a song or clip that will inspire a makeup look. When I find one, I sketch while I'm listening; I get in my zone and see where it takes me. TikTok has given me this amazing platform to tell stories, but there are also days when I just want to post with my beb or goof around with friends. I like comedy and TikTok dances, too. I love that freedom to be who I want to be in the moment. I can make a statement, shake things up, or just be my crazy self.

Creating content can take as little as a few minutes or as long as six hours. There's no clock ticking unless it's a sponsored post—then I have a deadline. Sometimes I will do a single stand-alone video and other times a series. In October 2020, I decided to do my thirty-one days of Halloween (I had done them the year before, too). Each look was another step forward in a story I wanted to tell. I knew the beginning and the middle when I started, but I didn't know where it was going to end. It began with stuff that was on my mind: I was having friendship issues with people who just weren't answering my calls or texts. The pandemic had made it hard for us to see each other and I wasn't doing the things that they were doing. I was trying to be responsible and smart (yeah, shame on me). So I did a really pretty makeup look and changed my eye color. I made my lips bigger and my eyebrows different and wrote, "Don't change for anyone."

The next video after that was titled, "If I Could Change, Would I?" It was a full clown look with hearts around the eyes, nose, and mouth, different hair, same contacts, me slowly changing into someone I didn't want to be. Then came, "I'm like a Glitch," a black liquid look. This was a reference to how people hate glitches, like ones you might see on TV. It was basically a message for my haters because at that time everyone was invested in my looks. Then I posted "Visibility" with black liquid coming out of my eyes. My eyes were blacked out and stuff was coming out of my mouth. It was supposed to be the old me dripping out of my face. I did a very creepy smile with long, sharp teeth and white contacts and captioned it, "All smiles here," which represented me playing a part I didn't want to play. The last video was a full clown look with my mouth stapled. That was me giving up, telling my bebes, "I can't do it anymore."

All of these looks were me sorting through my emotions, and that was one long and torturous therapy session. It was taking a lot out of me and I just couldn't go on with it for the whole month. I was trying to be honest and also give voice to other people's struggles. But I didn't really have a plan. Sometimes I sketched it, sometimes I didn't, because I was just so in the moment. I was going with the flow of my emotions, which scared me, because looking at my TikTok feed, they were all sitting there together. If you want to really understand me, look at my makeup, because I paint it all over my face. Sometimes it's a whisper, sometimes it's a primal scream, but the looks are always me saying *something* about what I am going through. The Halloween ones were me baring all in a way I'd never done before, probably because I was feeling so confused and sad, and it was my way of processing. Even when my face is completely made up, sometimes beyond recognition, I'm exposing myself, stripping myself down until my emotions are right there on the surface for all to see.

When I'm working on one of my looks, I get totally in the zone. I might close my door and not come out for hours. My family knows not to disturb me because I get nasty if they knock or make any noise. I hate to be interrupted and I do warn them: "Everyone, I'm doing my makeup. You know what that means." I shut the world out, turn off all the overhead lights, put on my LED lights and one ring light, and get to work. I've filmed the process a few times, showing the before and after and how it gets from one stage to another. I even posted a video in 2018 where I was crying in the middle of filming. It just had so much meaning and I couldn't hold it back. I thought my followers should see that and understand that I emotionally invest in each video. This is not just playing around for me; it's pouring my heart and soul out. It can be very intense and kinda terrifying, but I am willing to do it for me, for you, and for everyone who needs it. It's about my audience as much as it is about me. I don't own these emotions; we all have them.

The best part? After you put it all out there, after you let your art speak volumes for you, you can just wipe it off. That control comes in handy when the emotion is fear or anger or backstabbing betrayal. Just like that, it's gone. Makeup is therapy for me. It brings me to a place of peace, where I can tell myself, "I know what I'm doing." I'm connecting my dots, literally. Without makeup, I would probably just break down because I can't talk to people easily. I don't know why. I haven't figured that one out yet, and it's been forever. But makeup has given me a voice that is powerful and far-reaching. Some people write, some dance, some sing, some play an instrument. It doesn't matter what you do or what skill level you're at, everyone needs that outlet. Having a creative outlet can fill a big hole in your life and distract you from things that stress you out. Without makeup, I would be like my mom's pasta cooking on the stove with the lid on. If I didn't have an outlet, some way to take that lid off, I'd boil over and be a big, hot mess.

A lot of my bebes ask me, "What do I have to do to get a video to blow up?" or "What do I got to do to get famous?" For some people, yes, you get lucky and you blow up on one video. Then, hopefully, you can keep that up and build on it. But it can't be all about the views. It gets tired really fast. The answer is simply to express yourself, whether it's on social media or any other way, shape, or form—as long as you like it. Success comes from loving what you do. Not sure what you wanna dive into? Expose yourself to all sorts of possibilities. Try a bunch of things and see what sticks—it's as simple as that. It can be a hobby, a curiosity, a talent, or something that just brings a smile to your face. It doesn't matter what you do. Irish step dance, anyone? Pottery? Pancake flipping? Pokémon? My little sis draws dragons, and she is darn good at it, so there you go. Shanti has a positive series on her platform. She posts little videos of things that are positive, like sending gifts to residents in a nursing home. Anthony loves to play video games. My dad loves BMX bike riding. My mom loves to hike and be outside whenever she can. My aunt Hemali loves to cook and share her videos. Whatever you choose should inspire and excite you. You can take lessons or teach yourself—there are plenty of how-to videos that will break it down. You don't have to be Clown Girl (it's kinda taken . . .). You can be Dance Boy or Poetry Person or Nobody Knows and I Ain't Telling. Write your own narrative and character description. My point here? Find your fun and fabulousness. Don't overthink it; let it flow.

It's there. I see it in you, and I see it in me. Whenever I am feeling stuck or blocked, when I'm empty or on autopilot, I remind myself to dig deep and get back to the thing that makes me feel alive again. Clown Girl isn't all of me, but she's a keeper.

Run It Back: Who Needs a Creative Outlet?

We all do, trust me on this. Having a way to express myself is not just a fun distraction, it's a form of loving and caring for myself. Since I love and care deeply about my bebes, I want you to find yourself a way to channel your creativity. This is my advice on how to get started and the things you need to ask yourself on your outlet-seeking adventure. But YOU need to put what you learn into play, got it? Don't just answer, take action.

✦ What makes you happy? It's a simple question, right? What puts a smile on your face and brings you joy? My mom likes hiking, Dad is into biking, my grandparents like gardening, and Anthony loves fashion (like me). It can be something artsy or scientific; it might be cooking or redecorating your room. Think outside the box here; you don't have to be a painter or pianist, I know plenty of peeps who customize Air Force 1s, bead bracelets, or make smoothie bowls. I'm in awe of it all.

◆ What makes you "you-nique"? There is always *something* that is you and you alone, something that makes you an individual like no other. What do you do better or just plain *differently* than anyone you know? Explore those possibilities, because that's your special sauce. In a world of ranch and honey mustard, whip up your signature dip.

◆ What have you *always* wanted to do? Learn sign language (hello!), deep-sea dive, or star in a TV show? Lay the groundwork for your dreams and you will def find your outlet. Enroll in a class, get schooled on YouTube, and read up. Set the wheels in motion and you'll be on your way.

◆ What puts you at peace? Makeup makes me chill out. If I'm at my breaking point, I can pick up a brush, start doing my face, and the stress just melts away. An outlet is therapy; it literally lets out all your anxiety, worry, and wound-up feelings. Think about what brings you relief when you're revved up. There's a form of creative expression in there somewhere, I promise.

◆ What gets you fired up? The thing that makes your heart beat a little faster. The thing that gets you excited and gives you butterflies. That's a great place to start looking. My friend Riley gets a natural high from styling hair, I kid you not. Don't question it, just go with it, any "it" that amps you up.

On Avani

My mom, Anisha Gregg, says:

Avani has been through so much—more than most eighteen-year-olds. People think her life has always been perfect and easy, but that's not true. She was so devastated when she had to quit gymnastics. Even to this day, we can't talk about it, watch videos of her competing, or flip through pictures from her gymnastics meets without tearing up. It's a wound that's still healing. Selecting the photos for this book—all those photos of her in leotards on the floor and beam—brought back a lot of those memories. But even though it's painful to remember, gymnastics is so much a part of who Avani is, it had to be part of her book as well.

That's Avani—very strong and very practical. She pushes through any pain or discomfort, knowing there's something bigger and more important on the other side. She may try to hide it from me, but I'm really in tune with all of my kids' emotions. I can read them when they're sad or something's bothering them. When Avani started getting hate comments on her social media, I noticed right away that it was affecting her, eating at her. I told her, "Just block and delete. Get off the app, get off your phone, distance yourself from the ugliness." I was ready for her to just give it up altogether and go back home to Indiana if it was too much to take. I couldn't see why she would want to place herself in the line of fire. Then she looked at me, fiercely determined, and I knew that would be the end of the argument. She was not going to let anything or anyone take away what she had worked so hard to build. It's very easy to hate when you're hiding behind a screen. But Avani was going to make her content, and if people didn't like it, she would have to hear about it and not care. Luckily, Voni has never much cared what people think about her. She's her own person and she has never once worried about fitting in. She would much rather stand out.

Avani also has this huge heart, and her generosity truly knows no limits. She rarely spends a cent of the money she makes on herself. What she has, she wants to share. It's never, "Oh, this is all mine." She sees herself as working not just for her future, but for her family's—she wants all of us to be safe and secure. We all feel a little spoiled. Avani doesn't know how to say no to her siblings, especially Priya. They take advantage. "Voni, can I borrow this?" they ask. By "borrow" they mean can she give it to them, and of course she does, because she delights in making them happy.

Avani has always been a hard worker and known

the value of money. Between gymnastics and school, she never had time for a job during the year, so she worked as a lifeguard one summer. They paid her next to nothing, eight dollars minimum wage, and she was so proud of it. She's always wanted to be self-sufficient and that hasn't changed. I see the same little girl in her today. Avani may have blown up on social media, but she's never lost touch with who she is and where she comes from. You can take the girl out of Indiana, but you can't take Indiana out of the girl! She's still quiet and reserved and I have to pry things out of her. My other two, they can just talk away. I could ask one question and they'll talk for hours. Avani, I ask one question and it's a yes-or-no answer. With her, I have to look into her eyes or pay attention to her body language to read her, because Avani is not going to tell me if something is bothering her.

With all she's got going on, Avani realized she needed an assistant to keep her schedule and organize her life. She wanted to hire a stranger, and I thought, Well, that doesn't make any sense. I sat her down and asked, "What would you think about me quitting my job? It takes away eight hours of the day that I could be focusing on you and what you need. I could turn my full attention to helping you grow." As I explained it to her, I could just see how happy she was. She looked *so relieved and excited that I could tell it was the right decision for both of us. So I resigned from my job to focus on Avani and see where her career takes her. We make a great team, and neither of us would want it any other way. After all, who knows Avani better or loves her more than me?*

chapter five

Haters

I have this favorite quote that you might have seen on some of my merch: "If you don't love me, I love you." It's basically my way of declaring to all my haters (and there are many) that even if they aren't feelin' me, I'm going to still love them, no matter what. I really stand by that. I don't hate because what you give out is what you receive. So, when people are vicious on social media—when they post horrible, untrue things intended to hurt, embarrass, or cancel me—I do my best not to feed it. Haters gonna hate, that's the oldest and truest fact in social media. At the very least, I know I'm not alone. All my Hype House OGs and close social media friends have been on the receiving end. However, I think I win the prize when it comes to hate gone wild. I'll get there in a bit.

First off, let me explain that there is a difference between hate and bullying. Bullies are a more intense form of haters. They're the ones who keep coming back, the repeat offenders. They're relentless, and they seem to draw a big bull's-eye on your back that makes you the target of all of their internal drama, which is also something you should know: bullying is not about you; it's about them. Bullies feel the need to knock you down because of their own insecurities and self-loathing. They were looking for a way to feel better about themselves, and then you came along. This can amount to picking on you mentally or physically, or even making snarky comments that cause you to doubt yourself. Bullying can come from a stranger, an acquaintance, or even someone close to you—a kid, an adult, or even a group. Bullying comes in all shapes and forms, but bullies have one thing in common: the pain they inflict on their victims. From what I gather from my parents' childhood stories, our generation has elevated hate to a whole new level. We have taken it online, given it a worldwide audience of gazillions, and allowed it to hide behind an anonymous handle or a profile pic that looks nothing like you . . . unless you really do look like the clown from *It*? Not judging. Cyberbullying has many outlets. It can happen anywhere you interact socially online, like on social media, video games, texting, or group apps. It can be words but also images, like when someone purposely posts an embarrassing picture of you or shares info that was never intended for public view. It spreads lies, gossip, and general garbage about an individual just to cause hurt and harm. It's aggressive and it can incite more and more people to contribute, creating a mob mentality: "Get her!"

It's sad. Online should be a happy place where people are free to celebrate themselves unapologetically, connect, and share, but it's not. For example, I would post a YouTube video that was over ten minutes long and literally within seconds, there would be a couple of dislikes (thumbs-down). LOL, you haven't even taken the time to watch it, but you have your notification set on my videos so you can dislike it as soon as I post. That's just crazy and sad. Unfortunately, hate holds social media hostage, and it's gotten to a point where we've come to expect it. Joining the online community allows total strangers to say obnoxious things about the way you look, the way you talk, how you dance, whatever. It's totally understandable to me why someone would want to delete all their socials and fly under the radar. It's not a warm and friendly place out there.

I never used to be this cynical, but I got burned big-time. Now I know you have to be careful, you have to be aware, and you have to take it all with a grain of salt. Fan accounts and hate accounts coexist, and I guess you can't have one without the other. There are many fake and hate "Avani" accounts out there. I'm over 2 billion likes at the moment, but I've learned that the more likes I get, the more reasons bullies have to reach across cyberspace and take aim at me. Comment all the clown emojis you like—I am Clown Girl, after all—but I will do what I want to do without your permission or approval. Ask anyone who knows me and they'll tell you: I'm tougher than I look. You can't be in the business I'm in without developing a thick skin. If I took everything that people said or wrote about me personally, I'd probably be hiding out on some desert island, all faith in humanity gone. I'd be talking to coconuts and palm trees.

The source of the hate actually amuses me sometimes. Usually it's people who are mad at themselves and looking for an easy target. Hey, I am not live, and that show was recorded, so I can't answer you back. It doesn't get easier than that. You want to pop off, be my guest. Just recently, some adults actually commented negative stuff about my show, *Here For It with Avani Gregg*. My mom was so mad: "How could a father say that and post it publicly? Is that what he's teaching his own kids?" Honestly, I found the whole situation funny. A grown man is sitting there watching my teen content and hating on it. Do you not have something better to do with your time? Are you really that bored?

Most people feel bullied at some point; it seems to be a universal human experience these days. Personally, I feel like it's a song on constant repeat in my life. It's been going on since middle school, and I wish I could say it's gotten better, but it hasn't. If anything, it's gotten more intense because of my following. The thing that *has* improved, though, is how I look at it and how I tune out the toxic. At least I try to. Shanti will tell me, "Voni, don't take the bait." Sometimes I can't help myself, but I have made the conscious decision to be the better person, to look the other way, to ignore all the attempts to take me down. I envision this shield surrounding me, just repelling all that negative energy, and I practice letting the bullying bounce right off. That's right: can't touch this.

On my show, my friend Charli D'Amelio told me her crazy bullying story. Her first bullies were actually moms of kids she was in dance class with! Those grown-up (I use the term loosely) women told their kids to drop Charli as a friend because she liked to do hip-hop and their kids were all in ballet. I shook my head. Come on! They were anti-hip-hop? Aren't adults supposed to know better? Aren't they supposed to show kids how to be kind, inclusive human beings? Aren't they supposed to be teaching children to respect each other's differences? Guess not, or at least not with this crew.

That was a shocker, but I can top it.

I have gotten death threat DMs from total strangers. Not once, not twice, but countless times. Anthony, too. It started when someone messaged me, "I wish that you did not exist. I wish that you would just die." As if that wasn't enough, they sent detailed descriptions of *how* I should die, like by choking to death, getting hit by a car, or stabbed in the chest. It was a pretty long list. I had to take a deep breath before I responded, which in retrospect, I shouldn't have done, but I was so furious! I typed back, "I don't know who taught you this or how bad your life is going right now, but I don't need to hear it."

Anthony and I have both gotten so many of these that it doesn't even faze us anymore, and that's sad. Bullying should never be normalized, which is why I have to occasionally clap back. When I do, it's like a snowball effect and everyone jumps on the comment train. I get tons of people defending me, but probably the same amount (maybe more) say, "Chill! It's just a comment. It's not like they're going to do something." Well, it is doing something. I'm living a public life, and you can't just threaten it. Even if you don't like my hair, my nails, or the sneakers I'm sporting (yes, I've gotten hate on my footwear. I know, right?), that doesn't give you permission to publicly pick on me. You know when your mom told you, "If you don't have something nice to say, don't say anything?" Someone should pin that to all social media feeds as a reminder.

I also get hate when I choose to *not* say something on a subject. "Well, you have a huge platform, so you need to talk about the Muslim concentration camps that are happening right now!" I would love to, if I knew more about them, which I don't. There are so many issues and so many impor-tant causes to support, and I need to educate myself so I know about them. But even when I do, I may not be the best person to bring them to light. There are others who are wiser and more eloquent, and I defer to them. I am not an activist, but people think I should be because I have the numbers. They tell me what I should say and when I should say it, and that does not float with me. Push me and I push back. There is a nice way to share information or start a conversation without calling me names or accusing me of being anti this or that. There were times last year I found myself wanting to just give it up, all of it, because it was becoming too hard to please everyone. No matter what I did or said, I was met with meanness. When you keep coming up against that wall, you're bound to think, *Why bother?*

My friends and family rallied around me and reminded me that I couldn't quit because that would be letting the bullies win—and that's not going to happen. I have worked so hard to get where I am. It's my job to be a public figure on social media, but what I go through on the daily is pretty rare. People with normal jobs don't receive the amount of hate that I do. They don't have to deal with being attacked all the time. My life isn't my own because I live in the social media fishbowl, and that makes me question if this is really what I want to do for the long run. Does all the good (like my bebes loving and inspiring me) outweigh the bad (like the haters that come for me about everything)? I love what I do, but sometimes I really don't like it. Does that make sense? Maybe this will explain why.

In April 2020, my social media accounts were hacked. I didn't even know until one of my friends told me that someone was showing an inappropriate video on my TikTok account. Basically, the hacker had called my phone carrier and asked general questions about my bill. Once they got the representative to believe they were talking to me, they said that I had gotten a new phone and needed to switch the SIM card. Then they had free access to all my information. I mean *everything* from my socials to my parents' phone numbers. Usually when you get hacked, they spam photos and post stuff like, "Follow this page for a follow back." This started out like that, but then it got a lot more serious. The hackers posted terrorist videos on my Instagram and then TikTok, and they were sending links on how to sign up to be part of a terrorist group. Then they went live and showed very bad stuff, like videos of people being executed with machine guns. It was horrible, and I couldn't do anything to stop it. I had no control. When I finally got my accounts and phone number back, I had to apologize to millions of followers because they saw some pretty disturbing stuff on my accounts: "I'm back & I'm so sorry. I got 17mil [followers] and 1 billion likes on TikTok and I can't even enjoy that [right now]."

But it didn't even end there. My manager got a lot of emails from moms calling me out and asking how dare I post those videos on social media. Like, come on . . . really? In order to stop the hackers from going live, TikTok had to delete all the videos and drafted videos from my page. I felt so violated, and I really didn't know how to get back on social media without having this dark cloud hanging over it. I knew I hadn't done anything wrong, but I couldn't help feeling responsible for my fans being subjected to this nightmare. It was a while before I was able to post and not be afraid someone else would hack me again. In that way, the hackers terrorized me. They made me fearful to simply go about my business and do what I love. The only person who actually texted and checked in on me was Charli. "Weren't you scared they were going to hack your phone if you texted me?" I asked her. Everyone else was, even Anthony.

"Nope, I just needed to know you were okay," Charli told me. "I didn't care about anything else." She's one of the few who truly gets it because she's been there. When you're swept up in the hate, you feel like you're drowning. I needed someone to throw me a life preserver, and she did. Baes forever.

My mom was also amazingly cool about it. "If you're hurting, we're all hurting," she told me. "If they attack you, they attack all of us because we have each other's backs." But she was scared, really scared. It was such an invasion of privacy. The hacker was texting her and my dad personal messages that were terrifying, threatening to hurt us all. This went on for two weeks, and we were all so on edge. The doorbell would ring, and it would be the delivery guy, but we'd jump, thinking it was some kidnapper or homicidal maniac. It was *that* bad. I may be on social media, but I never wanted my family exposed. Despite what my mom says, I think it's unfair to them. I caused them so much stress with this situation, and I felt helpless. I couldn't do anything. I couldn't fix it. My mom filed a police report, but since the hackers used a burner phone, they couldn't do any further investigation. She also called our phone carrier and asked them to put us on the highest level of security available. Lesson learned. Then in January 2021, my manager was contacted by an investigator from Canada. They had caught two guys in their early twenties who had hacked a social media influencer in Canada. When they collected the hackers' laptops and equipment, they found videos and personal information of mine on it. They did the same exact thing to the Canadian influencer as they did to me, so the investigator strongly believed that they were connected to my hacking as well. My mom got in touch with him and shared all the information she had with him in hopes of putting the hackers in jail for a long time.

It was a horrible incident that could have torn my family apart. Instead, I think it actually brought us closer together. We all follow each other on social media and share everything. But when this happened, I think it made a lot of people in our friend circle and our larger family circle start to question what I do. They worry about my safety and how this life I've chosen will impact not just me but my parents and sisters as well. I think they've grown to accept it, and even embrace it, but it's been a big learning curve for us all.

When I first started getting hate, my mom freaked out: "Oh my gosh, Avani. You need to get off social media, you need to block those comments!" That was just stuff like, "U ugly" or "Hate that fit." "Mom," I pleaded with her, "do you know how many of these I get? If I blocked everybody who hated on me, that's all I would be doing." She still gets upset when I get hate comments and tries not to read them altogether.

I stopped reading comments for a while because I could get a million positive ones and still focus on the negative one. Some trolls tried to DM my sisters, too, and that is something I will just not take. You can come at me all you want because I chose this career for myself. But my sisters didn't ask for it, so BACK OFF. Shanti usually has to calm me down because none of this bugs her like it bugs me. She will let it roll, while I'm in full-on warrior mode.

Some people view my profession as an open invitation to say stuff about me. I chose to be a public person, but I never asked for people to hate on me. Bullies feel very bold behind their phones and computer screens. If they didn't have screens to hide behind, would they be that aggressive? Would they have the guts to say it to my face? Somehow, I don't think so. That's why cyberbullying is such an epidemic—it's bullying for cowards. They can shoot their bullets and we can't see where they're coming from.

Social media is a pretty intense line of work to be in. There are days when I want to crawl under the covers and not come out for like a week. Would that really be so wrong? In the beginning, I let it get to me a lot more than I do now. I took the comments to heart and questioned if I really was as ugly, stupid, useless, and untalented as they said. I literally had someone spam my comments like 100 times with "I hate you." I have no idea why. I never met them and I'm pretty sure that the cute little mirror selfie I posted wearing the teddy bear hoodie did nothing to provoke it. Now, I see it for what it is: jealousy, boredom, or a desperate cry for attention. They see how many people my platforms reach and they're like, "Yeah, I want a piece of that!" They think that by calling me out, humiliating me, or denouncing what I do, they will gain followers. Fat chance. My bebes will stand by me and shut them down.

Likewise, I will always defend someone who can't defend themselves. That's something my mom taught me. I will stand up for anyone. Even if I don't know them, I will jump in and set that bully straight. I've done it for people at my old school, I've done it for some some elderly women at the airport, and I've done it for friends. One time, these guys were bullying my friend's brother on the school bus every day. Finally, I couldn't take it anymore, so I stood up and told them to *Shut the F up!* and leave him alone *or else.*

I can't stand when people treat others with disrespect. No one is better than anyone else. We all walk this earth. We're all human beings. You may not agree with someone's opinions, but they are entitled to them, so don't try to "cancel" them for being different. I don't want to think of anyone being hurt the way I have. I don't want anyone to go through it. It makes my blood boil. What I'd like to tell the haters is this: Please don't dump your baggage on me. Breaking someone down and getting a reaction is not a cure for your issues. Don't go there, because if you do . . . you're just wasting your time.

Run It Back:
When Bullies Strike

On my Facebook show, Charli and I chatted with a therapist named Kati Morton, who took us through the steps of what to do when you're being bullied. I think our conversation puts things into perspective and explains what you can do to defuse the hate and protect yourself. Give it a watch, and if you need more help, check out these websites as well:

https://www.stompoutbullying.org

https://nobully.org

https://www.thetrevorproject.org

https://www.nami.org

Kati Morton, LMFT, Marriage & Family Therapist at https://www.katimorton.com

✦ Safety check: Are these just words, or are they active threats that you need to take more seriously? Snarky remarks are annoying and kind of pathetic, but threats should never be ignored. Either is cause for telling someone what's going on, whether it's a parent, a teacher, a coach, or the authorities. It's not "tattling" if someone is making you feel unsafe or upset. Bullies rely on you to be too intimidated to talk. They count on your silence; that's the power they have over you. Never hesitate to speak up. Simply telling someone shifts the control out of the bully's hands and into yours.

✦ Make real connections with real friends because bullying can make you think you're all alone and nobody actually cares about you. That's not true. Surround yourself with a support team because they will remind you of what's really important. Hint: it's not the haters!

✦ Build up your confidence (see chapter 10 for how to "do you" fearlessly!). It's hard for someone to destroy your self-esteem if it's rock solid. Negative words can only hurt you if you choose to believe them. Sticks and stones, bruh.

✦ Resist the urge to clap back. This is a big one for me, and it's something I'm still working on. If you give hate energy, it will only grow. Ignore it, block it, delete it. Whatever you do, don't respond. Your reaction is fuel for the fire. A bully wants to work you up and needs to feel like they own you. If that fails, they move on to another target.

✦ Tune out. If you're being cyberbullied, get off your phone or your laptop and limit all social media interaction for a few hours or even days. Remove yourself from the hate and don't check the comments (no matter how much you want to). Let things die down while you pull yourself away from the negativity. You don't have to hear it. I remember when I first started getting bullied, I handed my phone to my mom and said, "You hold this for safekeeping so I can't look at it." That didn't last very long because I cannot exist without my phone, but at least it proved that I had the power to walk away.

✦ Take the higher road. Don't bully back and don't give in to your anger or peer pressure to post something negative in reply. If someone slams you, the best response is to say nothing, I promise. You may be tempted to counterattack with hate, but that won't make things any better. At some point, we all have to realize how hate destroys everything good in this world. But not to worry, love wins, it always wins, it *will* always win. You can quote me on that.

On Avani

My little sister, Priya Gregg, says:

How would I describe my sister? Well, for one, her personality is very vivid. She has always been outgoing, whether playing in the backyard or simply interacting with her friends. People say we look alike. Personally, I don't see it. She looks like a beautiful human with a bright glow constantly radiating off her skin. I kinda look like a human who's spent time in a wolf den and just awoke from hibernation. I love her personality—the way she acts and how she doesn't mind what anyone thinks. She's one of the strongest people I know. Getting hate on the internet is something many people go through, but few know the effect it has on a person. Avani's been through it multiple times, but she stays the kind, funny person she is. That's just dope to me.

We have so many silly memories together. I re-member she collected these squishy little beads called Orbeez. They grow like ten times larger when you put them in water. We had a huge bucket of them and one time, when she went to pick it up, they spilled every-where in her bedroom. It was a huge mess. We spent hours picking them up while we were laughing be-

cause we kept slipping on the hard floor. In the end, our mom came in and threw them all out. Oh, well . . .

I spend a lot of time on video games, and when I say a lot, I mean A LOT. It's my joy, my entertainment, my escape from life. One time I got hacked, though, and I lost everything. I nearly quit the game and my guild because it was hundreds of hours down the drain. When I told Avani, she offered to help me. She bought me my dream item as a gift in the game that I can use all the time to advance, and I started up again. I don't know if Avani knows this, but her little act of kindness gave me a whole new role in that video game, and I will always be grateful that she didn't think it was just an unimportant game. She knew it mattered to me.

I'm really proud of Avani, as proud as any little sister can be. I love my sister and I love how far she's come. She proves that you can be a big success, get a lot of popularity and attention, and still stay the same kind, good person you always were.

chapter six

Body-ody-ody

*I*t's one of those days. I look in the mirror and the inner dialogue starts: *Gurl, no amount of makeup is going to cover up the bags under those eyes. Hold up, those pants do not make my waist look snatched. Why am I built like this? Nothing looks good on me. Wait, is that a ZIT on my forehead?*

That, bebs, is what goes on in a brain that's stuck in the dreaded body-shame spiral. Sound familiar? Come on, fess up, you know it does. Where does it come from? Personally, that's an easy question to answer. Try having millions and millions of eyes on you, and maybe a third of those people have something to say about how you look. There's lots of "QT" and "SLAYYY" and "Heather" comments that make me smile. But then there are the others, the ones that nitpick every hair out of place. Seriously, I wonder if they're sitting there looking at my post under a microscope, 'cause that's what it feels like. You just gotta point out one tiny little flaw ("It's the greasy hair for me!") and I'm triggered. It plays with my head, and soon I don't even need the body shamers to diss me—I can do it all by myself. I thought these shorts were fire, but you tell me they make my legs look weird, and all of a sudden I start believing it.

You don't have to be in the social media spotlight to have body insecurities. Most people struggle with them, even those sexy models who strut down the runway in underwear and angel wings. I think if I looked like that, I'd feel pretty darn good about myself, but then again, maybe not. I mean, even the most beautiful person on the planet dislikes something about their face or bod. I promise you, not even a supermodel feels confident 24/7; it's our nature, but the world we live in also creates unreasonable, unrealistic body goals. Distorted body images start on the inside: your mind develops this ideal of what is "attractive" and decides it's not you. It's anyone *but* you because you're so self-critical and convinced you can't measure up.

That warped vision can be triggered by almost anything. Maybe you look at magazines that have been heavily Photoshopped and compare yourself to those gorgeously glam models and celebs. Maybe you see people posting on TikTok and their skin is filtered glowingly smooth. Maybe you see this influencer on IG who is super fit with abs of steel, but you don't know if they edited in those abs by using an app or not. Then on the other side you have people who are completely open about their editing because they are doing it for themselves and not others. I got news for you: perfect human beings do not exist. That's what makes us human. Perfect is for those mannequins in the store windows—brainless and built of plastic.

When I was training as a gymnast, I felt like I was in good shape. I was getting in tons of cardio, stretching, and strength training, and I was eating right. I felt like my body was lean and mean. When I gave it up, things started to go soft. I wasn't good with it. That's when I began to hear a little voice of insecurity whispering in my ear whenever I posted a photo or video, or even when I caught my reflection in the car mirror. I was haunted by it. I would like to say that as I get older, it's getting a little easier to love myself and stop focusing on my flaws. There are days when I just don't feel like I look my best and will not film, but they're fewer and further between. Outfits definitely help. If I'm wearing something dope, it gives me a boost of confidence and swagger.

People on the internet love to call me out about my body shape, but I have to say, I'm liking it at the moment. I'm cool with not being anything but myself, thank you very much. What I don't like is my overbite. I still haven't made peace with the way my teeth look when I smile big. When I complain, people tell me I'm crazy, but I feel like it's *so* noticeable. I'm also really sensitive about my hip dips, those little curves below your hips and above your thighs, but they are easily erased with a little fashion magic. I'm able to style myself in a way that complements my body, which makes me insanely happy.

Our reasons for hating our bodies run deep, and I believe they need to be open for discussion, not dismissed. There are a million messages floating around in the universe that are just plain lies, and we absorb them day after day. "Your body isn't good enough." "If you don't look like X, you're ugly." How many times do we have to hear them and see them before we realize they're just preying on our insecurities?

I don't know about you, but I'm tired of being the victim. You can reject all that toxic talk, switch the narrative, and create a safe place for everyone where we see each other in a positive light rather than a negative one. It's not just about you, it's about future generations. Back in the day, everyone wanted to have an hourglass bod like Marilyn Monroe; she was a huge sex symbol and not a size 0. Then something shifted. This generation has pushed back. Have you seen Barbie dolls lately? They look more like real people, and that's progress. But change starts with us—the thoughts we think and the words we say, both to ourselves and out loud.

Positive Posting

Every time I glance at my feed and see one of the comments below, I smile. I hold my head up. I feel good about myself, and I carry that feeling around with me the rest of the day. Why not hit that heart icon and add one of these followed by a slew of starstruck emojis? What you put out there, you get back.

Queen! (Correct information has been detected)

Heather wishes she were you

Slay

Okayyyyy

I see you

Ur beautiful

Perf

Will the queen say hi?

So pretty ngl

It's the confidence for me

No hate, but next time please be careful. I have

asthma, and you just took my breath away with your beauty!

Icon

You're my idol

Prettiest person on the app

Every time I look at you I smile

The award for the prettiest person on the earth goes to . . .

I've figured out a formula for when I need a body confidence boost: I'll dress up fancy, do my makeup, and make myself look as stylin' as possible. Outfits that I put a lot of effort into instantly make me see myself in a different light, like a walking piece of art. I also feel empowered when I have my crazy long nails with designs on them. It's the tiny little details that spice up your look but also lift your mood and mindset. Anytime I'm really hating on myself, I turn my home into a spa and declare an Avani TLC day. I know what I need, and sometimes it's just a little pampering and primping so I feel pretty.

Love Yourself

Home spa check! Once in a while you need to love on yourself and take care of you.

Here is what I like to do at home to help me relax. Each time is something different, but you get the point:

- ✦ I like to massage coconut oil on my scalp and work it through the ends of my hair. Then I tie it up until I take a bath and wash it out with shampoo.

- ✦ I apply Ordinary AHA 30% + BHA 2% Peeling Solution on my face.

- ✦ I love a lip mask. Gotta have a soft, smooth pucker!

- ✦ While the peeling solution and lip mask are working their magic, I clean up my eyebrows and run a hot bath.

- ✦ Once the time is up, I wash off the peeling solution and take off the lip mask.

- ✦ Then I soak in my hot bath.

- ✦ Once I'm done soaking, I use an exfoliating scrub and shave my legs.

- After my bath, I use a Hydrogel Exfoliating sheet mask from Zitsticka.

- While I'm waiting on the mask, I put on a moisturizer and brush out my hair. Sometimes I like to put braids in it.

- Finally, I put on some comfy clothes and curl up in my bed and watch TV. Ultimate at-home spa complete!

There's been a lot of talk recently about what body positivity means. There's no clear-cut definition, so let me try to explain mine. From where I sit, body positivity is celebrating your body and others' bodies, no matter their color, shape, or size. It's a social movement that strives to affirm that we are all beautiful in our own way, and we don't need to change or alter ourselves to fit into some mold. People are even singing about it. In "All About That Bass," Meghan Trainor sings, "My momma, she told me, 'Don't worry about your size . . .'" Preach. Lizzo's "Juice" spells it out loud and clear: "Mirror, mirror on the wall, don't say it, 'cause I know I'm cute." Society should never dictate what we should look like or make us feel bad about ourselves.

That's a power play and it won't work. We know better, right? You and you alone should set the rules and
define what is desirable, hawt, cool, or cute. My definition could be way different from yours, and that's okay.
After all, not everyone likes to rock mom jeans. But I'm
positively me, and I own it.

The flip side of body positivity is body negativity,
and it can take its toll on your mental health. Body negativity is hating how you look to such a degree that it
hijacks your entire self-esteem. Body negativity creates an obsession that's hard to crack, and it can be
triggered by family, peers, or the world in general.
These delusions become cemented in your brain and
blow things totally out of proportion. You may actually
feel bigger than you are or imagine flaws that aren't
evident to anyone but you. They can make you super
self-conscious. Trust me, I feel this way when I post bi-
kini pics. In the moment I feel cute, but the photos have
to be exactly the right light, the right angle, and the
perfect pose. I practically twist myself into a pretzel to
look "natural." I know it's ridiculous and I look perfectly
fine, but I am constantly considering how that pic is
going to be scrutinized, shared, and commented on.
So yeah, that's a lotta pressure right there. I shouldn't
care; I should be comfortable and confident enough
to just put something on my socials because I like it.

Someone else's thumbs-up or thumbs-down shouldn't be part of the equation. But sadly, it is.

If you're anything like me, you've got some work to do because the body negativity is not going to go away on its own. But I think we can do something about this . . . together. Let's make a pact, okay? Let's promise to love and respect the skin we're in—love handles, cellulite, overbite, zits, and all. Let's put an end to the opinion shopping and approval seeking, because if you love what you're wearing and putting out in public, that should be enough. Let's treat our bodies well—maybe cut out some of the greasy junk food, get some more sleep, go for a walk or run, and just move in general. Let's try to knock off the negative talk, about our own bodies and others'. Can we appreciate each other not just for how we look, but for how strong, caring, and intelligent we are?

When I was back in my gymnastics days, this was so much easier to pull off. Whenever I mastered a new skill that took so much strength and ability, I could pat myself on the back. It was physical evidence of how awesome my body was. Now, when I'm lazing around thanks to the pandemic, I don't feel that way anymore. This "loungewear" phase doesn't help, either. I've been in these sweats and oversize tees for too long, and wearing a messy bun or baseball cap 24/7 messes with your head (literally). Sometimes I may be in the same clothes for several days, and the whole wrinkled/stained/needs-a-shower look is not a good one for me. Guys can pull it off, but I don't grunge well. That's the key right there: what makes Anthony feel good about himself might not do the same for me. So you have to figure out how to get comfortable in your body and what clothes, hairstyles, makeup, or none of the above allow you to feel that way. I give you permission to do some shopping or thrifting, borrow from your big sister's closet, polish your nails, and dye your hair any shade you like. Okay, if you're young, check with your parents first on that last one—my mom would have freaked if I was a few years younger and dyed my hair purple. Whatever makes you look in that mirror and shout, "Damn, I look good!" is a step in the right direction. So experiment with makeup, play with accessories, and don't let anything hold you back.

I'm working on stepping up my body positivity game and I believe we can all be on that journey—for our own mental health and so we can empower others to do the same. First off, surround yourself with people who build you up and tell you how beautiful you are, inside and out (helloooo @luvanthony). It also helps to talk about your feelings with other girls and guys—you'll be surprised to learn how common body negativity is.

When my friend Larray and I sat down on my show, we compared notes: "Same, same, same." Just hearing from someone who I look up to as a powerhouse of positivity made me feel validated. Even he hates things about his face and body and struggles with body negativity on the daily. It helped to tell each other we looked cute and laugh about how silly our self-doubts were. When I walked away from that chat session, I felt so empowered. No more bad vibes.

So let me throw some love at you: you're beautiful. I am not just saying that to be nice; I believe it and I want you to believe it, too. Love your body because it's the only one you have. Don't beat up on it. Stop shaming and punishing yourself for being imperfect. Imperfections rock. Why would you want to be a cookie-cutter version of everyone else? I stan a person who wears their differences like a medal of honor. Someone once told me, "You can't hate yourself happy." Truth right there. If you want others to love you, you have to love yourself and project the image of how you want to be seen. If you think you're bootylicious, you're creating energy for people to see you the same way. Body confidence is contagious.

That said, I have had total strangers come up to me and say, "Wow, I can't believe how confident you are." Their comments are usually in response to how

I look, what I'm wearing, or my crazy platform shoes. Sometimes, it's said with an edge, like being confident is a bad thing. Is "confident" code for "full of yourself"? If so, I'm not having it. As far as I'm concerned, confidence is key. You want to be anything? You want to go anywhere? You want people to take you seriously and not use you as a doormat? You have to buy into your own awesomeness. And you can't just say it; you have to embody it. I know it's hard to project body positivity all the time. My own has gone up and down like a yo-yo for years. But if you commit to it and catch yourself every time you start slamming the way you look, confidence will become a habit and you'll always have it in your back pocket so no one—including yourself— will ever be able to dull your sparkle. The best TikTok dancers have swag. As for those shamers, I wish I could sit them down and spell it out: when you judge someone by how they look, it doesn't define them, it defines *you*.

Run It Back: Say It with Me

These affirmations will get you on the road to loving yourself, 'cause I love you! Look in the mirror and tell yourself:

✦ "Dang, I look dope."

✦ "I am protected, well respected, I'm a queen, I'm a dream!" (Thank you, Yung Baby Tate.)

✦ "I will not compare myself to strangers on the internet. Period."

✦ "I came, I saw, I slayed."

✦ "I am fierce."

✦ "I don't want to look like anyone but myself."

✦ "I am who I want to be."

✦ "I am beautiful, no matter what they say." (Yes, Christina A.)

✦ "I am unstoppable."

✦ "Lookin' hot, smellin' good . . ." (Slay, Bey!)

On Avani

My friend Madi Monroe says:

Avani and I met at VidCon 2019. At the time, we had been following each other but we didn't really know anything about one another. We hung out at VidCon and I asked her to come stay with me in LA! Eventually she signed with my mom, who became her manager, and then stayed in our guesthouse in LA. Ever since then, we have been best friends. We share a lot of the same interests, but at the same time, our personalities are total opposites. I am very outgoing and say whatever is on my mind, while Avani is more introverted and thinks through every situation. I think this is what makes us a perfect pair.

Traveling is always so fun together. Going to Hawaii and the Bahamas was definitely the highlight of 2019 before the pandemic. We had the most amazing time and made so many crazy memories! It's been really hard not seeing her face every day. Not being able to hang out with your best friend is the worst, but Face-Time, texting, and social media keep us in touch.

Avani is definitely one of the most selfless and caring people I know. She always puts others before herself, even in extremely tough situations. She also puts so much time and effort into all her work. I think Avani is 100 percent the most creative person I know. She's hardworking and passionate, not to mention hilarious!

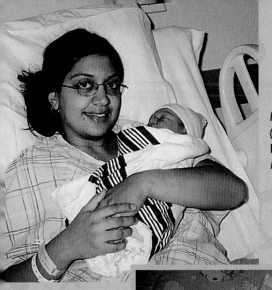

My grand entrance (with my mom), November 23, 2002.
Photo by Lewis Gregg.

Baby Voni, one month old.
Photo by Anisha Gregg.

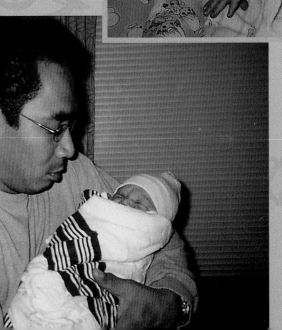

Daddy's little girl.
Photo by Anisha Gregg.

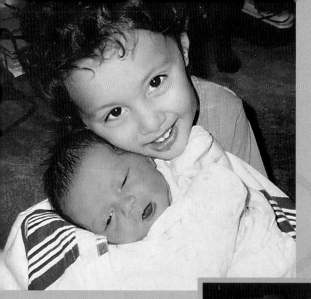

My big sister, Shanti,
was always my
number one fan.
Photo by Lewis Gregg.

I always had a
flair for fashion
(3 months).
Photo by Lewis Gregg.

Always smiling.
Loved purple since
the beginning
(20 months)!
Photo by Anisha Gregg.

First day of
kindergarten.
Photo by Anisha Gregg.

Sister Act: me (left), 17
months, and Shanti
(right), 3½, with our
first dog, King.
Photo by Lewis Gregg.

Dynamic Duo,
summertime.
Photo by Lewis Gregg.

And Priya makes three, 2006.
Photo by Lewis Gregg.

My fam going to an Indian wedding in 2006. *Courtesy of Gregg family.*

Christmastime 2010 (trying to convince Santa I was a good girl this year). *Photo by Anisha Gregg.*

With Pop-Pop and Na-Na on my second birthday.
Photo by Lewis Gregg.

With my Ba, Dada, and sisters.
Photo by Anisha Gregg.

I had a natural talent for gymnastics (age 7).
Photo by Lewis Gregg.

Dana Mannix gymnastics center

My very first gymnastics class at Dana Mannix Gymnastics (age 3). *Photo by Lewis Gregg.*

Shanti teaching me a handstand.
Photo by Lewis Gregg.

Ready to compete (age 8)!
Photo by Lewis Gregg.

Won so many medals over the years, we lost count (age 6).
Photo by Lewis Gregg.

Me with my trophy after a gymnastics meet in 2013, level 4 (age 11). *Photo by Lewis Gregg.*

Practice makes perfect . . . even at the Grand Canyon. *Photo by Anisha Gregg.*

Level 8 state meet in 2017. *Photo by Lewis Gregg.*

All makeup looks courtesy of Avani.

Where it all starts: my sketches.

Photos of sketches by Avani.

relationship

Oct 2nd 2020

inside yet out

Without words
I still express
the
feeling

ALL I CAN SAY IS THAT I
LOVE YOU SO MUCH. THANK
YOU FOR LETTING ME
WASTE YOUR
TIME
- THE ONE
YOU CALL
YOURS
<3

Oct 5th

the star of
the fake show.

My first Clown Girl look.

Mirror selfie with Charli.
Photo courtesy of Avani.

On vacay, from left to right: Chase, Charli, me, and Anthony.
Photo courtesy of Bryant Eslava.

Me with my girl, Riley.
Photo courtesy of Avani.

Me with Rowan, my Interactive Gymnastics teammate.
Photo courtesy of Avani.

Madi always gives me a lift.
Photo courtesy of Avani.

My hometown bestie, Lydia.
Photo courtesy of Avani.

Me with Katie (one of my gym teammates) at VidCon in 2019.
Photo courtesy of Avani.

Me with Chase Keith at Social Bash in Boston.
Photo by Shanti Gregg.

Clowning with my gymnastics bud, Gracie.
Photo courtesy of Avani.

My beb, Anthony.
Photo by Riley Hubatka.

Photo above and photo directly below by Bryant Eslava.

Photo by Riley Hubatka.

Winning my TikToker of the Year Shorty Award! *Photo by Anisha Gregg.*

My furry babies, Jack and Benny. *Photo by Anisha Gregg.*

Always there for me (from left to right: Mom, Priya, Shanti, me, and Dad). *Photo by Bryant Eslava.*

My dream car! *Photo by Anisha Gregg.*

chapter seven

Besties

*I*n sixth and seventh grade, I was part of a clique. I'm not proud of it, but it's a fact. I thought this group of girls was fun and cool, and definitely popular, so I looked the other way when they picked on some poor, unsuspecting girl's hair, voice, clothes, body . . . you get the picture. They were pretty toxic. While I was hanging with them, I had mixed feelings. Yes, I loved being part of the clique, but it also made me squirm when they did things I knew were wrong. I wanted them to like and accept me, but I was afraid that if I spoke up and told them to cut it out, they'd cancel me. Well, I was right about that last part. As for the rest, I should have known better because you're only as good as the people you hang out with. It was the little things they did that showed me their true colors, like not inviting me when they were going somewhere or taking cheap jabs at me. They would say something backhandedly nasty and I would ask them to please stop: "Well, that one actually hurt, and I told you before not to say that." That incentivized them to keep it up.

These girls weren't friends, they were frenemies, and I er found out they were laughing at and mocking me beh ny back. Seven years later, I swear I'm still angry with wanting to be part of the group. I was so concerned they would ditch me that I didn't listen to my gut, which told me I was better than this. Eventually, my friend Lydia and I finally saw the clique for what it was and decided we wanted no part of a pack that was flaming kids for fun. When I finally "unfriended" them, I became a middle school outcast, but it helped me figure out who I could really trust, and who was worthy of my loyalty and friendship. News flash: not the mean girls. Not even close.

After that, navigating social circles was like crossing a minefield. Gymnastics practice and meets meant I was MIA from all the "normal" social activities of middle and high school. Any friends I had were on my gymnastics team. None of them attended my school, which meant school became a lonely place. Most of my peers pretty much wrote me off and thought I was weird, and anyone I had been friends with before saw how busy I was with training and just stopped asking me to hang. Say "Sorry, I can't" enough times and that will happen.

Lydia was the only one who stuck by me. After our stint in that clique, we were always together in school and after, on the outside looking in, until we couldn't take it anymore. We decided to do online high school for sophomore through senior year. I said it was because I needed to focus on my gymnastics training, but TBH, the isolation was also a factor. It got to a point where I *had* to leave high school, even though I tried my hardest to reason, "Why should any of this matter to you? You don't matter to them."

That feeling of being betrayed by my so-called besties really stuck with me. It colored the way I saw potential relationships going forward. Once you've been burned, how do you know someone won't suddenly turn on you, ditch you, or dump you? How do you let people in your life if you're afraid of being lied to all over again? I admit it gave me some serious trust issues. As a result, I don't let people in easily. I hold back and put up walls. You wanna be my someone, my BFF, my beb? You want me to trust you enough to tell you my deepest secrets? You gotta work for it. Until then, I will fiercely protect my heart from getting torpedoed. It's taken a lot of fire in the past, and I'm not all that eager to risk it again. You have to convince me you're worth it because, sadly, not a lot of people are. And I have certainly not shown the best judgment in weeding out the good ones from the bad.

It's not always toxic talk or actions that cause besties to break up. I've seen how friends simply grow apart. Sometimes it's sudden, and other times it's a slow and painful death. I've had people come in and out of my life. At first, it makes me incredibly sad when they leave because we've laughed and shared so much of our lives together. Then POOF, they're history. It feels like someone has died. I never existed, *we* never existed. It's a really hard lesson to learn, but friends don't always stay friends, even if the times you spent together were the best. People drift apart for so many reasons: time, distance, disagreements, or distrust. Sometimes your interests change and you just have nothing in common anymore. Lydia left school for seventh and eighth grade and we drifted apart for a while. Then she came back in ninth grade and we saw each other in gym class. We started talking, instantly became best friends again, and from then on, we've been ride or die.

I accept that friendships can go through growing pains, and you can take a pause if you need to. Real friends will find their way back to each other. But when it's just not working, when you're compromising yourself to keep the friendship going, when it's causing you stress and sleepless nights, it's probably time to cut ties. Try not to agonize. I have spent so much time and energy searching for reasons to stay friends with people and trying to convince myself it was salvageable when I knew it was already over. One of the reasons you may be clinging to a friendship is that you're afraid of being lonely. I get that because I've also considered that a compelling reason to keep holding on. But I've given it some serious thought, and I think I'd rather be stranded on a desert island than be tethered to a fake friend. You won't be lonely for long, I promise. And in the meantime, you got me!

The good news is that experience has made me an expert at spotting the warning signs when a relationship is about to implode. I have had people say they're my friends, only to turn around and use me to gain clout. I've been ghosted by guys who said they were into me. I've had friends who cancel, stick me with a check, start bossing me around, or try to one-up me. Friendships should never be hard work, and (red flag!) they should never hurt.

I've chased people to try and keep them in my life. That's me—I don't like conflict, and I always want to make people happy. But after a while, you need to ask yourself if *you're* happy. What are you getting out of this? Is the relationship a one-way street? Are you doing all the heavy lifting?

I love when people try and use me, too, pretending we're tight when it's been years and all they want is something I can give them. Case in point: I've had so many people text me and Snapchat me on my old account that I don't use anymore: "Hey, miss you so much." I'll answer because I've seen people do trends on me where they post screenshots of me "being rude" by not answering them. Doomed if I do, doomed if I don't. I'll reply politely but fakely, "Hey! How are you? Oh my gosh, it's been so long" and they message back, "Yeah, I just wanted to see how you were doing."

This conversation could go for thirty minutes before they get to the real reason they're reaching out: "Does David Dobrik send you merch? If you ever have any merch that you don't want, just send it over and I'd be so happy to have it." Or they'll ask, "You have Addison's phone number? Charli's? Can I have it? Do you have this actor's Snap? I saw you post with him. Please, please tell him I looooove him!" I just sit there for a few minutes, shaking my head in disbelief. Bruh, you do realize you were the one who started all those rumors about me in middle school. You tried to ruin my life, just sayin'. Instead, I take a deep breath: "Sorry, can't really do that. But have a nice day!"

Here's another example: There is this set of people who don't stop talking about me on social media because when they use my name on a TikTok, they usually gain followers. So they claim we're BFFs, always have been, always will be. Stuff like, "Story-time: I went to school with Avani and she was my best friend!" It's delusional. We're besties, huh? LMAO.

Real friends don't expect anything from you. You have to weed out these users and abusers. All I can say is friends are the best . . . until they're the worst. When a toxic friendship happens, letting go will set you free. Who needs that in their life? Still, ending a friendship doesn't necessarily require a big, dramatic confrontation or even a formal letter of dismissal. Save your breath and just slowly let it slip away while you stop texting, calling, or making plans—kind of like a gradual ghosting. Maybe that's the wimpy way to go about it, but like I said, I hate conflict. So I just phase them out. It might feel weird at first, but if they're not really noticing (or caring) that you're out of the picture, it should tell you something: you're better off without them. I've also been on the receiving end of this when a close friend stopped answering my texts. Okay, I can take a hint. Thank you, next.

Which brings me to a happier subject: good friends, great friends, and friends who mean the world to me because they make me feel loved, whole, and insanely happy. That circle gets smaller and smaller as I get older, just like the collection of vintage clothes in my closet. I'm editing down my friend list. Now I'm more interested in quality over quantity, and my idea of what makes a bestie has evolved, too. It used to be just someone who would invite me to sleepovers or share their Sour Patch Kids. Now it's someone I can call at three a.m., who is my emotional support animal (LOL), and who would bail me out of jail without asking why I was arrested. I need thoughtful, patient, reliable, real friends who are ready to go to bat for me. Of course, it's a two-way street. I've been there for my peeps as well. Case in point: Lydia was going through a hard time with personal issues a while back, so I decided to fly her out to LA for a couple days. We didn't even go anywhere. We just sat in my room watching TV and talked that whole time.

Lately I've been feeling lonely, so my friend Riley and I constantly talk and text to pass the time. We tell each other, "Okay, it's just another day. We're just waiting until we can see each other again." She was planning on coming down here with her family for a bit to stay at Newport. I told her, "I will drive the two hours to see you just to spend a few hours. I need my Riley fix!" Good friends have that "cure-all" magic that heals your heart. They also help you put things into perspective. Riley and Lydia will tell it to me straight without making me feel bad. They don't judge me, and they accept me for who I am even if they have different styles, opinions, and stuff going on.

They know how to have fun and they love to laugh with me, not at me. They want the best for me, they are protective of me, and they are committed to standing by my side. Even when the going gets tough, they don't get going.

To my friends (you know who you are), I say, "Back at ya." I am so grateful to have you in my life. Finally, my bebs, you are my besties in so many ways. You are the people who follow me, shout out your love, and make me want to be better because you believe in me. If ever I'm feeling lost or lonely, I have you to lift me up. How did I ever get so lucky?

Run It Back:
A Real Friend . . .

✦ Celebrates Y-O-U and all you do. No judgment, no jealousy, no jabs behind your back or in front of your face. Way too many former friends got all hot and bothered as soon as I started to blow up. If you throw me shade, I'm going to show you the door. Period.

✦ Won't bolt if things get messy. Instead, they will support you, cheer you on, and help you mop up. When I was dealing with my phone being hacked and the resulting hate storm, *sooo* many "friends" stayed far, far away. When things were back to normal, they expected to just pick up where we left off. Yeah . . . no.

✦ Laughs at your jokes and isn't afraid to get loud and crazy. This is a big one for me. I need someone who gets my goofy and will roll on the floor, cracking up till it hurts. My sense of humor is an acquired taste, so liking it earns you a spot on my team.

✦ Is 110 percent trustworthy. Opening up isn't ever easy for me, so my closest friends understand that I need our convos to be just between us. Friendship should be a gossip-free zone.

✦ Has a sixth sense or telepathy when it comes to knowing what you need. Seriously, I don't have to say a word because my besties read me like a book. I can just look at them and they'll bring me an acai bowl (thanks, Mom).

✦ Lets you cry ugly tears on their shoulder. They're not afraid of seeing you a stressed-out, sobbing wreck or mad if you leave mascara stains on their fav shirt. Go on, let it all out.

On Avani

My friend Lydia says:

Avani and I met during our very first year of middle school, when we were eleven. We had a couple of classes together and we just hit it off right away. I asked, "Hey, do you want to come over for a sleepover?" and that was the start of it all. We lost touch when I was homeschooled for the next two years, but I remember seeing her start up on social media. She didn't have that many followers at first, and the kids in the neighborhood would try and trash her: "Oh my gosh, she thinks she's so famous." I can only imagine how it was in school for her. I went back to school during my freshman year of high school, and right away, our friendship was the same thing as sixth grade. We had one class and lunch together, and we would hang out after school every single day. Sometimes I would go over to her house after she got home from gymnastics, sleep over, and go to school in the morning with her.

The first time she really blew up we were on vacation in Florida with my family. We were in our bunk beds at night and she almost dropped her phone. "Dude, I just hit like 180,000!" I was like, "What? You hit what?" We jumped up and down and started screaming our heads off. We were fourteen at the time, so it all felt so surreal. When she got recognized on the street, we just looked at each other in disbelief: What in the world is going on? This was pre–Clown Girl, and Avani was doing the sign language thing and a lot of makeup directed to Twenty One Pilots.

We both started online school sophomore year. We transferred out together because Avani wanted to focus more on her gymnastics. I told her, "No way, you're not leaving me here." A lot of stuff went down with a bunch of different people freshman year, and I felt like she was the only one who understood me. All the drama brought us closer together and made us able to talk about super-serious things. We vowed we'd always have each other's back.

When we were younger, Avani always had this very unique style. She would dress up every single day for school, never wearing the same outfit twice. Neither of us had any money, so she would just thrift all her clothes. You would never in a million years think what she picked up could be a cute look, but she saw something in it, something no one else saw.

Over the years, Avani has changed in a good way, the best way. Now that we've both matured, she's definitely more accepting of herself and doesn't worry what people think of her. She was always original and genuine, but now she really celebrates that in a very positive way. When we're in the same zip code, we just spend all of our time together. Even if we can't go out, we don't care. We swim in the pool, watch Netflix all day, and enjoy real quality time. You know you have a friend for life when you can just sit around and do nothing and it's the best time ever.

The thing I love most about Avani is her loyalty. She's there for me 110 percent, no matter what. If I call her with a problem, she'll sit with me for hours and just talk about it. She never gets annoyed, even if it's the same problem over and over again. She always ends the call with, "Keep me updated," and then she'll text me a few hours later, "Are you okay?" So I know that even if she's far away, she's always there. Her ability to empathize is superhuman; she can always put herself in my shoes and understand what I'm going through.

She's also one of the funniest people I've ever met. She goes crazy sometimes, and I just love that. She can seem quiet and reserved, but once she trusts you and is comfortable, she's so outgoing, hilarious, and loud! Beyond all that, she's incredibly humble and real. She *never thinks of herself as famous, and if I point it out, she just brushes it off. In so many ways, she's the same goofy, emo kid I met in sixth grade, and I think that's why people love her so much. With Avani, what you see is what you get.*

chapter eight

Hearts

*P*oor Anthony. The kid had no idea what he was getting himself into when he slid into my DMs. We both have our versions of how we became a couple, mine being the *legit* one, of course. Anthony insists I ignored him the first time we met in person, but that's not how I remember it. Hey, we can agree to disagree on the backstory, but the one thing we agree on is that we have been together since March 2020, and it just keeps getting better.

It's pretty rare for me to talk about our relationship at all. We decided we were going to deal with it our way by keeping things between us and out of people's mouths and the media. No need to overshare and blast it across the internet.

I see lots of social media couples go through such drama—breakups, make-ups, and major Twitter wars. We were determined that would not be how we went about this. Ain't nobody's business but our own! We stand by that, but I couldn't write a book about me without including my beb. I can picture him reading this now, getting all red in the face because he thinks I am about to embarrass him and get all mushy, and he is right.

Before I met Mr. Anthony Reeves (aka @luvanthony), I wasn't really a person to let down my walls. I still don't, not really, because I don't know what walls I have up. But Anthony understands, and he likes that about me. Go figure. I'm a woman of mystery! That said, he doesn't need me to explain everything. We have this unspoken secret language and Anthony can just tell what I'm thinking from the tone of my voice or my facial expressions. No one in my life has ever caught on so fast. That's something really special, when someone just gets you and you don't have to work so hard because the connection is *there* naturally from day one. It immediately put me at ease and made me feel safe. By not pushing, nagging, or issuing ultimatums, and by accepting me for who I am without ever questioning or judging, Anthony made me fall for him . . . hard.

Our beginning, though, was kind of complicated. We first started DMing on Instagram in June 2018. Anthony followed me first when we were both posting fashion and barely had any followers. Then he posted something about being in Kentucky. I was just about to go there for a gymnastics camp, so I reached back out. I look at our conversations now (yes, I saved them all) and it's so weirdly random: "How'd you find your style?" and "Where do you shop?" Short messages, back and forth—just silly small talk. It got a little strange, and I guess we weren't hooking each other's attention. Then, around February 2019, it just stopped cold. We stopped interacting on Instagram, texting, everything. He had a girlfriend from his school and he was taking her to prom. Meanwhile, I was going to prom with Jaden. Jaden and I had met on social media and went as friends. Sometime after prom, I saw on social media that Anthony had broken up with his girlfriend.

The following October, months after he'd gone radio silent,

Anthony reached out once or twice. I think I replied: "Hey." That's it. I thought that was the last I would hear of him. Shoulda known better because the boy is hard to shake. We had both been at these two events, one in September and one in October. This is where our stories differ drastically: He says that at the first event, I walked right by, paid him no attention, and gave him the cold shoulder. He even thinks he said hi and I ignored him and shoved right past. For the record, I believe this is false. Dude, I didn't even see him! But then we were at another event and I waited in line at a meet-and-greet to take a picture with the Sway boys. We had both blown up on social media at this point, but I acted like a fan and stood there thirty minutes for my turn. Then, when I got up to Anthony's spot, I posed with him and made him feel very awkward. Again, there was no exchange of words at all. It was like our online flirtation had never happened.

A month and a half later, we had another encounter. I was really good friends with Bryce Hall and Taylor Holder before either of them blew up on social media. I was always at their house, and Anthony, who was friends with Bryce, flew down to stay over. When I would go over there, I did not see Anthony once. He was living there, so either he was avoiding me by locking himself in his room, or I just had blinders on. Once when one of the boys posted a TikTok with me, Anthony commented: "She's mine." But he never actually spoke to me. I remember I sent a screenshot of his comment to my friend Riley. "Okay," she told me. "You need to find out if this man likes you."

Nice idea, but who knew when I would have the opportunity? I finally saw him at Halloween. I was at Taylor's house, doing all the boys' makeup and hanging out with some friends. Believe it or not, Anthony was there, but again, I swear I never saw him. I took a video on my phone and, when I watched it back, there he was right behind me. We actually rode to the party in the same car with everyone else. The party was at this house someone had rented, and there was a big living room with long couches. I remember sitting down on one. I was just keeping to myself because I was new to LA and didn't like to socialize much. Just then, Anthony came along and sat down next to me. I don't remember what the conversation was or who started it (def him), but it was probably just some random stuff to break the ice: "You know this one? That one? You been here or there?" It was really awkward at first, but then we didn't leave each other's side for the rest of the night. We walked around together, and everyone was whispering about us. Addison Rae was there, and she told me she had been waiting for this moment to finally happen. When she was around the guys, she would always text me to let me know, "Anthony won't stop talking about you!" I didn't understand it. "How is he talking about me? We don't talk!" But apparently, I had been on his mind, a lot.

Once we started talking, we realized we knew everything about each other from our texts way back when. We talked through the entire party and had our first kiss that night. You are not getting more details than that, but let's just say it was nice enough for us to start hanging out every single day until we both went home, me to Indiana and him to Kentucky. I remember looking at the meet-and-greet picture I took with him on my phone and thinking, *So this is when it started*. I wasn't sure what "it" was just yet, but on March 7, 2020, he asked me out.

Anthony's my first boyfriend—unless you count some little boy from elementary school, a middle school crush, or this one other person on social media, but that did not go down well. It was a bunch of lying and then a good ghosting. But Anthony and I were friends first, good friends. We spent a long time talking, getting to know each other, and figuring out what we were about as individuals before we ever coupled up. I love how protective he is. He stands up for me time and time again, without ever being asked. He's my hero.

I never knew what it could feel like to have someone willing to fight for you. Anthony didn't either because his past two relationships were a mess. Each girl cheated on him with one of his best friends. Taking a leap was hard for both of us, but we had already laid the groundwork. We figured out early on that we had the same interests. We went to a concert together and realized that we liked all the same music artists: Billie Eilish, Tyler the Creator, Frank Ocean, Juice WRLD, X, Mac Miller. We like the same fashion brands, like Golf Wang, Billie's merch line, Saint Laurent, and Louis Vuitton. We stalk smaller brands that are from Instagram and some of the bigger Japanese brands. And we have never, ever argued (not once!), which is just crazy. I don't want to jinx it, but we always manage to put out the fire. It gets to a point where we know we're about to argue over something very little and we defuse it by turning it into a joke. Or we both just go silent for five minutes because we know that it isn't worth fighting about. I have a temper, so this defusing the tension is all very new to me. I think there is mutual respect and care behind it. We never want to hurt each other, not even a teeny-tiny bit.

When we compare our relationship to those of other couples, we realize how lucky we are to have found each other. I think it works because we spent a long time in the getting-to-know-you stage—years, really—and now we're living perfect.

During quarantine, Anthony was at my house with my fam

almost every day. People warned us, "Oh, you'll get tired of each other and become like an old married couple." But with Anthony, it's never boring, and I think because of how chaotic our lives are, it won't ever get boring. Not that boring sounds bad to me; I could just be happy chillin' on the couch with him forever, watching movies. We're both homebodies, but I also like to surprise him for his birthday, Christmas, and Valentine's.

I'm usually the planner and gift-giver in our relationship, the romantic one, but it does switch back and forth. People ask me to name the sweetest thing he's ever done. I think it's literally every time I see him. He is always attentive, cuddly, and my kinda crazy. There was this one time when all the boys were going on this trip to Texas. It was when I was nominated for the TikToker of the Year Shorty Award, and he told me, "Sorry, I'll be away for the whole week." Not gonna lie, I was hurt, but I let him go without a fuss. Then he surprised me by flying back to LA. He was waiting in my apartment when I walked in, ready to watch me win my Shorty. It meant everything and spoke volumes about how he takes our relationship seriously. He put me above everything, even his own fun and friends, because he knew what the award meant to me. I really don't need little gifts all the time. That day, his presence was the greatest present.

Some couples have a tough time saying the "L" word. Not us. We've been saying "I love you" since before we were formally dating. It was like two or three months in. I don't remember who said it first, and Anthony will not tell me. He likes to keep it that way: "Doesn't matter who was first, it was a really good moment." Then he gets all soft and cute, making me think it might have been him. We have nicknames for each other; I call him "Ant," "Anfony," and of course "Beb." He calls me "Bebe." I joke that one day we'll launch a clothing brand, Beb & Bebe.

People ask why we don't have any issues, why some couples constantly feud and we've been good for a year plus. I think it boils down to respect, trying to be mature, never being jealous, competitive, or shady. Honesty is a big thing for us. I don't want him to ever hold back or sugarcoat what he thinks or feels. If he's unhappy, I'm unhappy. Period.

It also doesn't hurt that my family is crazy about Anthony. My sisters love him, especially Priya because they both love gaming and Pokémon, so they have a lot to talk about. Priya recently got him a Pokémon card set as a gift. The way that Anthony geeked over it just made her day, and I had to listen to "He loves me more than you!" for hours. My parents know he's good for me too. When I won't spill to them, Anthony's got it covered. They helped me plan Valentine's outside our house, setting up a little picnic blanket and movie screen, and we ordered in from Mastro's. Anthony ordered the New York strip, lobster mac 'n' cheese, and a Caesar salad while I ordered a petite filet with garlic mashed potatoes. For dessert, my mom made us strawberry shortcake with vanilla ice cream. It was so yummy! I got Anthony this cute little film-roll photo album with a bunch of pictures of us, a royal-blue Venus et Fleur flower box, and these BE@RBRICK Dr. Martens boots that he'd been wanting for so long and couldn't find. He got me this humongous rose bouquet that was shaped into a heart (insanely adorable!) and two vintage Louis Vuitton items: a snap-on bracelet and a coin purse. I love anything vintage and had never seen anything like them. They are so freaking cute!

We celebrated our first anniversary a few weeks later by staying in an Airstream trailer at Joshua Tree. I planned the whole thing. It was parked in a remote area, in a private lot, with an outside bed swing and firepit. It was so relaxing; we could just be chill and watch the sunset. We packed a cooler (I had made lasagna and peanut butter sandwiches and brought hot dogs to grill). It truly felt like we were the only people in the world. This year, we have grown so close. I think we've been to-gether every day except for the times we went home to see our families. And whenever we *were* apart, I missed him . . . bad.

Mom's "Love-ly" Strawberry Shortcake

My mom's strawberry shortcake was the perfect sweet, romantic dessert Anthony and I shared during our outdoor Valentine's picnic. Mama for the win!

1 quart fresh strawberries, stems removed and
    sliced
¼ cup white sugar
6 mini sponge cake dessert cups (or one sponge
    cake loaf cut into slices)
Cool Whip whipped topping
Vanilla ice cream

1. Place the strawberries in a lidded container (lid off). Add the sugar and mix to coat. Cover tightly with lid and refrigerate overnight.

2. Place sponge cake cups on a serving plate. Top with strawberries, followed by a scoop of ice cream and a dollop of Cool Whip. Serve immediately and enjoy!

 # The Birthday Boy

I love surprising Anthony with one-of-a-kind, just-us-two experiences. For his birthday, I rented a house in Malibu and planned a little party with him and my family. On the actual date, I took him to Sugar Factory for dinner and then surprised him with a party at his house with all his friends, because he hadn't been able to see them much together. He was loving it, and I had to pull him aside because I knew he had no idea about the long drive ahead to Malibu. "Okay, wrap it up, Beb. Gotta leave in ten." I needed him to pack a bag for two days.

"Nah," he said. "I think I want to stay, since all my friends are here." Everyone knew what I had lined up, so they were also trying to get him out the door. I tugged at his arm: "Let's go, trust me, we *need* to go!" When I finally got him on the road and he saw what I had planned for us, he was just blown away by it. All of it. He'd never really had a big birthday like that. It was his nineteenth, though, and I thought it was about time.

Do we ever get on each other's nerves? Well, yeah. He says I suck at texting, which is so true. He hates when I don't answer back right away . . . or ever. My pet peeve is when I order him food delivery and he falls asleep before he can eat it. It happens all the time, and I am left holding the tacos. But I'm not gonna hold it against him. There are way too many things we love about each other to sweat the small stuff. Neither of us plays games, and that's a huge reason why we work so well as a couple. I'll ask, "Do I annoy you? Even just a little?" and he'll say, "Not even if you try."

Aw, nuf said.

Run It Back:
Love 101

Want your relationship to go smoothly? Here are a few pointers on what you two should do:

✦ Praise you like I should. As Fatboy Slim sings, "I have to celebrate you, baby." Instead of picking on the stuff you don't like about your significant other, shout out what you do like: his goofy smile, the way he wears his baseball cap backwards, or how polite he is to your family. Thank him when he does something thoughtful without your nagging. Compliment her when she looks cute. A little love goes a long way.

✦ Learn to listen. Seriously, it's the key to a solid relationship. Sometimes Anthony will just hear me out for hours. He won't judge. Instead, he'll let me go off until I feel better or run out of steam. Awesome boyfriend: check!

✦ Be honest about everything—you should have no secrets between you. Once you establish trust, it takes things to a whole new level. I think the best part of our relationship is how much Anthony and

I trust each other, and that comes from a willing-ness to share our thoughts, our feelings, and our past. I'm so brutally honest that sometimes he'll say, "Whoa! TMI!" Well, you asked!

✦ There are lots of ways to love. All are equally im-portant when it comes to keeping your relationship strong. There's romantic love (candlelight, roses, chocolates), compassionate love (respect, care, empathy, understanding), playful love (flirting and fun), and unconditional love (no matter what). What I need depends on the day, but I would never say no to any of them. Gimme gimme!

✦ Steer clear of socials. An occasional cute post is okay, but I think anyone who details their love life on the daily is just asking for trouble. If you're in a fight, never broadcast it. The Twitterverse doesn't need to be in on your dirty laundry, know what I'm sayin'?

✦ Keep the friend group out of it. In our case, that's tough because we're literally friends with all the same people. But if you're old enough to be in this relationship, you should know that asking others to weigh in and take a side is immature. Keep it separate from your social life.

✦ Respect each other. That's a biggie. No sliding into another girl's DMs, no complaining to her friends or fam, and no flirting with some hottie you randomly meet. Your relationship should be sacred, and you need to treat it as such. Honor bae . . .

✦ Give it some space. Yes, I wanna be around my beb 24/7, but I also know he needs to see his boys and have a life outside of our relationship. Resist the urge to smother, cling, or make unfair demands of his time. If you love him, set him free . . . occasionally!

On Avani

*M*y beb, Anthony, says:

Everybody in LA, all the social media kids, they're just jumping into love. They're lonely, nobody has nobody, and they're on the lookout for somebody to latch on to. Yeah, that's not gonna last, especially if you rush into it. The difference with Avani and me is that we took our time. I got to know her deep and literally took ten months to ask her out. I wanted to be sure that she's my person, the one I want to be with, and I thought she should be certain, too. Then we could go from there and everything would be good. Take it one step at a time and you get out of it what you put in. All the work pre-dating set us up to connect on a higher level.

The way we met might be up for debate, but I think it might have been at the Juice Krate tour. I walked over to her and the guy she was hanging with. I already knew her because we had texted on and off for two years. I was like, "Oh hey, Avani, what's up? Nice to meet you," and went in to give her a hug. She just looked at me and walked right past, didn't say a word. I was like, "Dang, this is messed up!" I was actually mad. After that, I was talking to the boys about her, even obsessing a little. Then we connected at that party and it was smooth from that point on. We're young, so a lot of people ask, "How can this possibly last?" Obviously, I hope it does, because, well, she's Avani. It doesn't get much better than that.

If you ask me what I love about her, I will say literally everything because there's not a thing that I don't love about her. She's funny. She's gorgeous, obviously. She's outgoing and so smart. There's really nothing that I don't like. Avani will try her hardest to annoy me, but it doesn't work. I think it's cute. As for what I do that annoys her, well, I would say the way I eat—the crumbs get all over the bed and she gets mad and tells me to clean up. I'm a dude, what can I say?

It helps that we have a lot in common, including the same taste in food. Avani likes her McDonald's a lot so that's a basic. I've been trying to eat more spicy foods lately because her family's Indian and everything they eat is on fire! When it comes to movies or TV shows, I never ever, ever watch anything unless I'm with Avani. We watched all of the Harry Potters together, and I'd never seen them before. We watched all of the Hunger Games together, too. We've watched a bunch of random little-kid movies. And then we've watched all of Family Guy and Rick and Morty. Our sense of humor matches up perfectly. I love hanging with my friends, but she knows I will always put her first. They don't mind; they're like, "It's cool. I'm happy for you." They've got their girlfriends, too, and I'm always getting them in trouble. The girls will complain, "Why don't you treat me more like Anthony treats Avani?" I put them to shame!

Don't tell, but Avani makes it easy for me. All I want is to see her smile, and that's pretty good motivation right there.

On Avani & Anthony

My friend Riley Hubatka says:

> Okay, my best friend has been dating this guy for so long, and I absolutely love him. I think they bring out the best in each other. They have one of the healthiest relationships I've seen out of couples our age living in LA. Avani always makes sure I feel included in whatever they're doing because I'm single. Normally, it would be conflicting to hang out with her when she has a boyfriend. Most other couples would shut me out. A friend would tell me, "Well, I have plans with my boyfriend. Sorry." But no matter what they are doing, I can be a third wheel with Anthony and Avani. They always welcome me and make me feel included. It's not like I'm hanging out with Avani and her boyfriend; I'm hanging out with the two of them and we're all friends. That says a lot about who they both are: confident, kind, no-drama people who want to make everyone in their lives feel special.

chapter nine

The Hype

*M*y Hype OG days feel like ancient history. We've all grown up so much since then, but the Hype House will always be a really happy memory for me, and the place that started it all! Basically, the Hype House was a content collective, with fifteen teens renting out a Spanish-style mansion at the top of a hill with a big gate outside. There was a huge pool, a hammock, and lots of stone terraces that we used as backgrounds for filming. We kind of announced it all with a hashtag and that built the buzz. Then we were interviewed for the *New York Times*, *Entertainment Tonight*, and the *Today Show*. Pretty surreal for a bunch of kids between fifteen and twenty-one years old, huh?

This is how it all started. I was friends with Chase Hudson, or Lil Huddy. We were just hanging out one day and he had Thomas Petrou, the guy who runs the Hype House, come over to take our pictures. Thomas used to do photography before he got into YouTube, and shooting influencers was his thing. I remember them talking about Hype and starting the whole thing up. Two weeks later, they signed the lease. The concept was to give a group of talented kids a great space as a backdrop for content—Thomas described it as living in a movie set—and the ability to be together without prying eyes Interrupting the vibe. The original name for it was supposed to be House of Olympus, at Chase's suggestion. But Alex Warren came up with Hype and everyone voted for that.

Ironically, I was one of the last people invited to join the Hype House because Thomas said he was scared I was going to say no! Besides me, there was Alex Warren, Kouvr Annon, Daisy Keech, Charli and Dixie D'Amelio, Addison Rae, Nick Austin, Patrick Huston, Ondreaz Lopez, Tony Lopez, Wyatt Xavier, Ryland Storms, Connor Yates, Hootie Hurley, and Calvin Goldby. At some point, I think I lost track of who was coming and going. People would visit from out of town, stay with a friend for a few days, and contribute to the content. The group just kept getting bigger and bigger, because if you were a popular creator, you wanted to be in the mix.

TBH, even though there were six bedrooms and huge common areas, we did most of our shoots in the bathroom, don't ask me why. Good natural light and an overhead, I guess? Beyond that, we liked the living room because of the high ceilings and the balconies, and because they looked cool on camera. I remember the pool was always freezing and we mostly used it for shoots, not to enjoy or relax. I mean, think about it, we were each pumping out three to five videos a day; that's like seventy-five to one hundred across all of our platforms daily. That's an insane amount of work.

If I had lived at Hype, I would have never gotten any homework done. Still, it seemed like I was there every day from the moment Chase and Thomas put the deposit down. Alex, Thomas, Daisy, and Kouvr lived there full-time, and Thomas was kind of the house manager. We came together as friends in the beginning, but we were also putting together a business. It wasn't just a party; it was a really creative environment designed to produce amazing content. There were rules to follow, and Chase was always on the lookout for someone who would fit in, scouting talent on social media. Basically, you had to be young, creative, energetic, and a little weird. That was the ideal!

The family bond between us was strong, and I made some friends for life in that group. We fought like family, too, but at the end of the day, everyone loved each other. Since I wasn't living there, I kind of kept my nose out of all the drama. I would take off, go back home, and get a report on it. Most of the time, it was just silly stuff: "Who left their acai bowl on the kitchen counter and didn't clean it up?" Speaking of the kitchen, no one ever cooked—it was Uber Eats and Postmates all day long, sometimes twenty times a day!

In the beginning, Charli was just fifteen and living back home with her family in Connecticut, so she would just come to LA to film with us. She was blowing up at the time, so for her, Hype was a safe place. I think we all felt that way, like we could just be ourselves there and not worry about being "spotted" or exposed. I was the only one who did makeup, so that made me a little unique. But I could also dance, be silly, and do comedy or pranks. No one there was gonna judge me. When I left, it started a lot of gossip: "Did Avani get kicked out? Did she walk away? What went down?" The answer is: nothing, I was just ready to stretch my wings a little. I found it exhausting to keep going back and forth because I was living at home, and I thought it was time to move on. Charli and Dixie had already exited, the pandemic was just starting, and I had to be quarantined somewhere. So it made sense.

As much as we tried to keep everything on the down-low, fans and paparazzi managed to find us. Our address got leaked because people reverse-googled pictures of the front of the house and found it on Zillow. That's when crowds started showing up, pushing the gate open, and just walking up to the front door. One time, these two boys drove up and stole some of our packages. They would come literally every day, trying to get in. Finally, they made it right up to where the mail was dropped. A mutual friend saw them posting on their socials, "Avani's shoes for sale," and sent it to me. I was like, "Are you kidding me? That's my property you got there! Give it back." Eventually, my friend convinced them to do the right thing and return our packages, but that wasn't the last time something freaky happened. On three separate occasions, someone followed my car when I was leaving for the night. I had a little Mini Cooper that I posted with one time, and they spotted it and trailed me until I got back to my apartment.

There was plenty of hate, too. People called us "cringe-worthy" and tried to roast us. They also labeled us as spoiled, aimless kids with nothing better to do with our lives. That couldn't be further from the truth. I took it all really seriously—we all did—and when I look back on it now, I see it as a time when I had a big growth spurt in my career. I know when the guys were coming up with the name for the house, they considered what the word "hype" stood for. It means intense promotion or publicity, something you put out there (like "hyping someone up"), or the buzz you get from being on everyone's radar. If someone has the hype, they're cool; if they lose it, they're irrelevant. But I also saw it as a responsibility. If I've got your ear, I'm going to use my hype in a positive way to entertain, make you smile, or draw attention to subjects that matter. In the TikTok universe, hype means excited or exciting, which is definitely true of my time at the house. It's funny to me how

Hype was all I could think about when I was in the thick of it, but now, I struggle to recall all the little day-to-day deets, conversations, and even the content I made there. It's all a blur, which must mean I have truly moved on. But I'll always be a part of it, and it will always be a part of me.

Run It Back: Rules for Being on Social Media

Ever since I've been on social media, which is a long time now, I've been very aware of the responsibility that comes with it. Even if you don't have millions of eyes on you, you're entering a very public space where whatever you put out there is up for public view. I'm eighteen and I've made mistakes, but these are the rules I live by:

✦ Watch what you say. Be sensitive to a lot of topics because you just don't know who's following you, what certain people have gone through, or the complexities of the situation at hand. Think before you post, period.

✦ Apologize if you make a mistake. You're learning and mistakes will happen (they've happened to me more than once over the years). People may still come at you, no matter how much you say, "I just didn't know and I'm really, truly sorry." Learn from it and do better next time.

✦ Don't overshare. Understand the consequences of putting everything—and I mean everything—

out there in the cyberverse. Once that content is up, it's very hard to get rid of. Even if you delete it, people can screenshot and share. Anything that would tarnish your rep or embarrass you has no place on your platform. Rule of thumb: if you wouldn't want your grandma to see it, it has no biz being on your feed.

+ Play it safe. Keep your passwords to yourself and don't post private info like your phone, address, personal email, or license plate. Make sure to check things like location services and advanced security if you're paranoid (um, me!).

+ Don't overdo it. Check your screen time. If you are spending twenty-three hours of the day online, it's time to cut back. You may love your device, but it won't love you! Wouldn't you rather be spending time connecting with *real people* instead of scrolling through the For You page? Consider taking a break and a breather, and maybe getting some blue light glasses. Time for a tech detox.

+ Avoid online drama. No need to jump on the comment wagon if someone is stirring the pot. If you can't keep your cool or your head, put down your phone. I am always so tempted to respond, especially when someone takes a jab at me online. Shanti tells me to count to ten and think before I clap back. Is it really going to solve anything? Is it going to defuse the situation or just make things worse? In the heat of the moment you may be tempted to type, but it's always better to be unproblematic.

✦ It's not all about the numbers. Don't become so obsessed with how many people are following/liking you and your posts that nothing else matters. If you want to grow, stay true to your content and it will come naturally. I also don't recommend buying likes, views, or follows. Stay the course, build good content, and collab with like-minded creators. All of the above will get you there.

On Avani

My friend Charli D'Amelio says:

Avani and I first met at Madi's house. It was October 24th, 2019. I'm really good with dates of significant events that happen in my life, and that is one I'll remember forever. I had always thought Avani was super cool and talented, but I was a little intimidated by her at first. She gives off that cool vibe that can be scary if you don't actually know her! We started hanging out because we had a lot of mutual friends and we were all in similar situations at the time. Eventually, we realized that we would make really good friends, so we started to hang out with each other a lot more and we just clicked.

Avani is calm, creative, and talented. She's a great friend to different people for different reasons. We're good friends because we look at life in very similar ways. We can both be a little shy, but we are outgoing when we are around the right people.

Our trip to Hawaii for Madi's birthday is one of my favorite memories with Avani. It was so much fun! We went scuba diving and just swam all day. It was one of the best trips I'll ever take. I admire her talent so much as a makeup artist. I wish I could be nearly as good as her. I'm trying, but I don't think I'll ever be on her level.

chapter ten

Do U

*E*veryone wants to know one thing about social media stardom: How can I get famous? My answer is always the same (and you can quote me on this), "Just do you." That response usually gets a few eye rolls because it sounds ridiculously simple or like a cop-out. Do people expect me to wave a magic wand or something? I have no idea how I got this "famous" this fast, except to tell you I have always been myself, 110 percent. There's nothing easy about that; authenticity takes guts and commitment. It requires unbreakable, unshakable confidence and dedication to your personal brand. It's something you can't fake; followers can spot a phony from a mile away and they will not take kindly to your content. You want to gain people's trust? You want to keep them coming back for more? Show them who you are and be legit about it. So yeah, I'm Avani, all the time. You may like me, you may hate me, that's your prerogative and I won't take it personally. What bothers me is when creators copy other creators' work without giving them creds. There are a lot of clown girls out there, just sayin', doing my exact looks and sounds. I don't believe it's cool to copy or purposely change who you are for whatever's trending. What's that going to get you?

Maybe more followers at first, but in the long run people will figure out you're not the real deal and it will come back to bite you. If you are "inspired" by someone's content, then duet it or give them creds where creds are due. Authentic means true, genuine, and—let's not forget—original. Authenticity is not just a quality you want to possess; it's something you need to embody. I have never cared what people think about what I post, how I dress, how long my nails are (yeah, they will even pick on that).

Even in middle school, I did my own thing in my own way and expressed myself through my personal style. I was exploring, figuring things out, and learning to assert myself. Now, I see it as a mini identity crisis of sorts—I was playing with what felt authentic to me and trying things on for size, literally. You would not have found many kids my age rummaging through bins and racks at Goodwill, but I would thrift every single day with my older sister or Lydia, and we would just go crazy, sometimes spending up to $50–$100 on piles of old clothes. Once I had my treasures, I would take them home and do a little repurposing. I might work on scrubbing out a few stains, trimming a tee into a cropped top, or patching a pair of ripped jeans. I got a rush from it and I literally never wore the same outfit to school twice. I would get some stares and snide remarks when I strutted down the halls, but I felt so in my zone. This is 100 percent who I am and I love it, so take that.

I seriously prided myself on paying for clothes by the pound. It was an entire process: gloves, mask, sweatshirt with the hood up. We had to wear the gloves and mask, not because we were in a pandemic (this was way before that started), but because everything was so dirty and dusty. All these items were coming straight from people's closets, attics, and garages and were old and not washed. The items were not safe to handle.

As I got older and more popular on TikTok, I didn't want to be spotted on my thrifting missions, not because I was embarrassed, but because it would take me away from shopping to stop and say hi or take a photo with someone. I didn't have much time to thrift, so I was methodical about it. I had a schedule and a system to stick to: I had to search each and every bin, go up and down each and every aisle, or I might miss something. Shanti would laugh. "Do you seriously need another dirty old tee shirt?" But need and want are two very different things. Each shirt became an extension of my personality and something I wanted to project on the day I wore it: edgy, funny, or fierce. The holes and stains just gave it more personality. Each item allowed me an opportunity to create something out of nothing. Before I got seriously into makeup, this was my art form. Even today, I will go with Anthony to the Melrose Trading Post on a Sunday, and we will go through every single booth, combing through them. We always find the best vintage jeans and jackets and all these cool tee shirts. I've gotten to know a lot of the vendors, too, and I love talking fashion and art with them. I earn a lot more now than I did when I was living in Indiana, so I can afford new and pricier clothes, but there is something about thrifting that reminds me to never lose touch with the old me. Thrifters are a breed unto ourselves. We appreciate the possibility that might be buried deep down in one of those bins. When I find something that speaks to me, it's literally like I've just won the lottery. My palms get sweaty, my stomach flip-flops, and my mind races: *OMG, is that what I think it is? Where have you been all my life?!*

Of course, I've gotten way better at thrifting, and my style has shifted. I would say 2018 was all about a mom jean layered outfit with a cool belt. I could always find belts, flannel-lined jean jackets, and huge oversize tee shirts at the outlets. In 2019, I started searching for higher-end stuff. People would throw away their old Burberry jackets and their old vintage Polo shirts and I would be in heaven when I saw a little pony logo or a piece of plaid poking through a crowded rack. Send them my way! The same goes for old vintage bags, shoes, and jewelry. Now I know that the items they keep behind the counter on the big glass shelves are more valuable. That's where I usually start, scoping out those rare finds. I know what things cost and if I don't, I'll research them so I know whether it's a deal. I'm also an expert at haggling and I find it fun to bargain with a vendor. It can be like tug-of-war, but I always win.

Lately I've been scoping out vintage Gucci alongside plainer items that I can layer, like basic crop tops and stuff like that. My style is a real mix of high and low. If I ever passed a Plato's Closet or Goodwill Outlet, I'd be down for diving into the bins of donated goods. I'll also comb through Etsy, Depop, Poshmark, and any other online retailers that sell used or repurposed items. I think these items have character. They each have their own backstory, and now I'm adopting them and weaving them into mine. I will always grab a funny shirt because it makes me laugh and is just so . . . unexpected. My favorite one says "World's Greatest Grandpa" on it, and I wear it proudly. It's so ridiculous to see an eighteen-year-old girl walking around with it on, so it makes other people smile, too. I also feel very strongly about shoes. They transform an outfit, so the wilder and crazier the better. You see a pattern here? I don't care if on Wednesdays we wear pink; I'll probably be decked out in purple. When I talk about authenticity, it literally covers me head-to-toe. My wardrobe may not be for you, but that's okay, it suits me to a (grandpa) tee LOL. 😊

My car is another way I express my uniqueness. It's custom, one-of-a-kind, and there's nothing else like it out there. It's a Fiftieth Anniversary Limited Edition (#18 out of 70 built) 2020 Dodge Challenger, and the color is Hellraisin, a gorgeous metallic purple. Backstory: Anthony, my dad, and I went to a dealership to test-drive a basic white Challenger. My previous car was an itty-bitty Mini Coop, so I needed to know if I could handle something bigger. After all, I wasn't prepared to sell my old car and shell out money for a new one if I didn't feel comfy behind the wheel.

"What do you think?" my dad asked. He was completely convinced it was the right choice for me. I caressed the steering wheel. "I love this car. It's perfect. So much room. And heat settings!"

"Well, is this the one you want?"

I shook my head. "No, it has to be purple, and I want a starlight ceiling with orange embroidery, and I want the rims a different color. I want a crazy car, but not too crazy, just a little crazy. Does that make sense?" He's my dad, so of course it made sense to him. He knew I wouldn't settle for anything average, and I wound up driving *him* crazy with my long list of demands. We wound up going to West Coast Customs, where they're used to crazier people than me asking for the impossible.

"What did you have in mind?" the salesman asked me. After I spelled it all out, he sighed. "That's quite a job, and we have a very, very long list of cars that we need to get done before we can get to yours. I'm sorry, it could be a while." But my birthday was coming up, and I really wanted to buy my own car as a gift from me to me!

My dad put his arm around me. "They'll try, but no promises, Voni. You'll get it when you get it. The best things are worth waiting for." West Coast told me to come back in a few days to go over more details because, apparently, my crazy was crazier than most. When I returned, the salesman got out my file and began to go over it, item by item, asking me if I was 100 percent sure. Maybe there was something else I would consider? Another color? Less detailing?

"Hmmm, we have this Challenger that we've been working on that I can show you," he told me. "Just so you get an idea of what yours *could* look like." I crossed my arms over my chest, prepared to stubbornly stand my ground. Ain't no one talking me out of my car. They opened up the doors to the showroom and it had the exact purple with the matte-black Challenger brands ready to go. I gasped. "Oh my gosh, that's it! That's *exactly* it. I want this exact car!" In my excitement, I missed the fact that the windshield had a sign on it: HAPPY BIRTHDAY!

"Um, this is your car." He laughed. "Your mom and dad planned this for a long time. They wanted to surprise you." I started crying and freaking out. It was everything I wanted, and then some. My dream car was right there in front of me, ready to drive right that second. It had custom Lexani wheels, WCC graphics with the logos in the headrest, my signature embroidered on the center console, and, last but not least, a starlight headliner. It was just *sick*. My parents know me so well!

Of course, like everything, when you do your own brand of "different," you have to be prepared for people to react. I guess I knew my Challenger would get looks, but not people attacking me. Literally, my first drive out, I got car hate. Is that even a thing? Apparently it is, because there are tons of car geeks out there who feel the need to share their opinions. I got a V6, and all these old dudes are very particular about their V8s. That's nice, but I'm not planning on racing you, even if you dare me.

Maybe it's not your dream car, but it's mine, so could you just let me have that? People will literally stop me on the road and pull up next to me and try to get me to race them.

That first day, I went to the gas station to fill the tank up and buy a charging cord because my phone was about to die. I came out, and there were these guys in a white van taking pictures. *Great, wait till they see the little girl driving it*, I thought. I hid inside the station for a while, but eventually got back in, locked the doors, and was so distracted that I didn't notice a car backing out in front of me. He rammed his car into my rim, dented it, and just took off. The guys in that van got a good laugh out of it. I was so upset that I started to cry. I had another guy pull up next to me at a light, roll down his window, and start cursing me out and flipping me off. I didn't know him, I didn't even look at him, but he saw a seventeen-year-old girl with bedazzled sunglasses in this custom car and it set him off. It always seems to be some forty-year-old with a chip on his shoulder, but I am not going to apologize for my car. Nor am I going to apologize for who I am. If Anthony is with me, he won't hear of it and will stand up for me. If the color or the glitter on the rims rubs you the wrong way, that's on you, not me.

My big plan is to collect custom cars—the more unique, the better. I don't want to be driving around in the same fancy cars as everyone else in LA. For my next car, I want the ugliest car you could probably think of, like an old Mercedes that I can paint dark brown with a light pink interior. I also want one of those small pickup trucks, the really awkward-looking ones, in white with custom pink flames on it. I just want weird, funny cars that no one else has. Because guess what? I'm like no one else, and I own it. That's just how I am.

Thrifting 101

*I*f you're curious and want to try thrifting, here are my tips for finding treasure:

✦ Clear your closet first. Not only will you make room for your new scores, but you can also sell your gently worn stuff to a consignment shop or resale site and make some cash to fund your first thrift. Check out thredUP, The RealReal, Poshmark, Depop, eBay, and Tradesy for selling and buying.

✦ Goodwill has good finds, especially the outlet, where you can get stuff by the pound and whatever people donate is just dumped into the bins. Nothing is labeled or priced, so it's a real search for buried treasure. My heart just races when I walk through the door: What will I find hiding here today? So much fun, and many of my fav items came from my daily visits in Indiana. To find a location near you, check out https://www.gwoutletstorelocator.com.

✦ Stay focused. Thrifting can be overwhelming and intimidating—so many racks, bins, boxes, and rows to rummage through. Walk around once or twice to get a feel for where things are, then devise a plan, like "I'll start left and work my way right." Lydia and I would sometimes divide and conquer, knowing exactly what each of us was looking for and shouting when we found it. Also, it's a good idea to keep a list or spreadsheet of what you want. You can even organize a Pinterest board to help you keep your eyes on the prize.

✦ Weekdays are less crowded than weekends because more people are at work or school. I also recommend going early before things have been scooped up or picked over. And, in general, I find small towns have more reasonably priced items than bigger cities like LA. So research a few good thrift stores to pop into when you travel or visit other towns.

✦ Learn your labels. A vintage Diane von Furstenberg wrap dress is worth more than one from Abercrombie. The vintage fashion guild has a website you can quickly hit up on your phone if you find something you think might be valuable: https://vintagefashionguild.org/label-resource.

- ✦ Make friends with the store staff. That way, they'll tell you when they restock or mark things down, and maybe even give you a heads-up when something you've been looking for comes in.

- ✦ Dress for instant try-ons. Most thrifting venues don't have dressing rooms, and sizing, especially on older pieces, can be so random. I recommend a tank top and leggings so you can easily pull things on over them.

- ✦ Shop off-season. If it's a hot summer day, you might find a rack of cashmere sweaters or wool coats for close to nothing.

- ✦ Look for details that say "quality." Lining in a jacket, shoes that are 100 percent leather, not "leather upper," natural materials versus synthetic. You can also easily spot things like delicate stitching, covered buttons, piping, and metal (not plastic) zippers. If you inspect items closely, you may find a real diamond in the rough.

- ✦ Scope out the flea markets. They're more accessible in LA than they were in Indiana. I love them because there are so many vendors and it's nice to support small businesses. Most of the stuff I find is handmade or vintage designer that's well-preserved. It can be pricier than hitting up a Goodwill, but the quality is worth it. Plus, it's really nice to wander around on a Sunday, talk to artisans, and see other people's originality on display.

On Avani

My friend Nessa Barrett says:

Avani is so beautiful and talented. She's one of the most genuine and down-to-earth people I've ever met. We met for the first time at a social media event last year. Since that moment, I've thought she was the sweetest. She has such a great heart, and there is so much passion behind what she does. She also works so hard. She is one of the only people I'm able to open up to. I can tell her anything and everything. She cares so much about others and will be the first to do whatever she can to make you smile the second she sees you're sad.

Once, we went on a trip to Joshua Tree for a weekend with a few friends. One day, while everyone was playing games outside, we wandered off together and walked around the desert on a path we found. As simple and boring as walking might sound, we joked and created stories from literally nothing. Most people would probably think we were crazy if they saw us dancing around and laughing, but that's why I love having a friend like Avani. I can truly be myself around her, and even when there's nothing to do, we have so much fun!

chapter eleven

Headspace

No matter how many followers I have, or how many friends are texting and DMing me on the daily, there are days when I feel incredibly alone. In those moments, it's as if I'm not part of the world around me. It's a total disconnect, and it creeps up on me, usually when I'm stressed and overwhelmed. Once it's there, that loneliness makes itself at home and becomes my obnoxious roommate. I wish she would leave, but she's way too comfy and not very keen on packing up.

Like so many people, the pandemic has not been good for my head, thank you very much. It's pulled me out of the scene, so to speak, and I've lost friends because of it. This new normal—let's just call it what it is, isolation—put me into full-on loner mode. Yes, I dealt with sadness when I retired from competitive gymnastics. And yes, bullying made me feel excluded. But this is a different kind of despair. This one made me feel guilty, like I was masquerading as someone else entirely. I felt like I was wearing a mask all the time, which is ironic, I know, since I'm known for painting my face beyond recognition.

From all appearances, there was nothing bothering me, despite the fact that 2020 was the worst and *nobody* (unless they were completely oblivious) was in a good mood. In my posts, on magazine covers, and in interviews, I was the happy girl just vibing and having the time of her life. I thought that's what I had to be because that's what people expected of me. I thought my followers wouldn't like me anymore if I stopped being all fun and games and clown makeup. But deep down, I was hiding a dark secret, and it was bubbling up to the surface. You want the real story? Behind the scenes and screens, I felt like I was lying to everyone, including myself. But let's take it back a bit. After all, this is my mental health *back*story.

It all started in late summer or early fall 2020. I'd already been through several months of the pandemic, watching all my plans for 2020 vanish into thin air. In a nutshell, it was a total washout. I was doing my best to keep on keepin' on, posting on all my platforms, following through with brand collabs, arranging virtual interviews and shoots, deep diving into this book. On top of all that, I was finishing my online high school courses—graduation at last—and coming up on my eighteenth birthday. I continued putting stuff up on my socials, but something felt *wrong*. Fake. Phony. Full of it. I was smiling on the outside, but inside, my heart was aching and my brain was struggling to make sense of all the chaos. I looked just fine, but I couldn't deal with life, which—given what I do and how crazy the world is—was very stressful. It was like I had to separate and become two different people: the one watched by 30 million pairs of eyeballs and the one crying into her pillow at night. Who would want to be around a Debbie Downer? But there I was, even with all the attention my career was bringing me, feeling horribly, desperately alone. The truth is, you can be in the middle of a huge crowd, surrounded by noise, and still be all by yourself.

Don't get me wrong, I'm very, *very* grateful for everything, but too many times, I've thought to myself, *It would be so much easier to just quit social media. This is too hard!* And when those thoughts come into my head, they send me running to a dark place where I doubt everything. My instinct is to simply check out. I couldn't tell you why; it's not like there's something that specifically triggers it or something I can point to. It's not linked to a certain activity or time of day or even a conversation. It just *happens*, and when it does, I am *not* okay.

There, I said it. I want everyone to know that it's okay *not* to be okay. I think we need to normalize it and cut each other some slack. No matter how great your life is—and mine is pretty great—there are times when you just get stuck in your head and it's hard to get unstuck. Honestly, I'm a person who could probably use therapy, but I hate talking about my issues. I worry that a therapist might give me an answer that I don't want to hear. So, where does that leave me? Usually wrestling with my problems on my own. When something's going wrong, I won't speak about it unless it's doing an insane amount of harm to me. My stubbornness kicks in and I announce that I can handle it myself: "Thanks, but no, thanks. I got this." And that's what I should do, right? I mean, I'm eighteen, and I'm supposed to be "adulting."

Well, that's what I used to think. I used to believe that admitting I was struggling made me a weaker, lesser person, and I was "a baby" if I couldn't figure out how to fix stuff on my own. But talking things out with friends and people I trust made me realize that's not it at all. It actually takes a lot of courage to reach out and ask for help. It takes a lot of strength to want to feel better and take steps to make it happen. Admitting you're not okay doesn't make you a baby; it makes you badass.

Many of my influencer friends have been down this same rabbit hole. I think it comes with the social media territory. We want to please our followers and make everyone feel good. But I've learned that when I'm not okay, I can't "put it on" or act like I'm having a party on my posts. I have to express my true feelings in my content, even if it bums some people out or isn't what they have come to expect from me. You might comment, "wasn't here for this," and I guess that's your right. Just respect that I'm trying to put myself out there and share with you guys. I need your support and understanding just like you need mine. I need to be real.

It took me a long time to figure out that communication is key. If you ask my friends and family, they will tell you I am the worst at returning texts. I leave a lot of people on read. I literally haven't seen some friends in over a year and I feel like the distance, both physical and emotional, has driven a wedge between us. TBH, it's mostly my fault. I'll see the text while I'm editing something, but I hate to get out of my zone and lose my train of thought, so I just put the phone on Do Not Disturb and the text just keeps getting pushed back further and further. Eventually, friends give up on me and stop texting altogether. Then I wonder where everyone went! My mom says relationships are like plants that need watering. You can't neglect them or they dry up, wither, and die. So I have to remind myself to check in. In a pandemic, absence does not make the heart grow fonder, it makes people think you're blowing them off and don't care. My bad!

When things started to ease up a little over the summer and I could actually meet up with my crew, I was a basket case. I had such social anxiety, and it came out of nowhere. I'm shy, but I'd never felt afraid to walk out on the street. Seeing someone moving toward me had never sent me running. I guess I had been alone and socially distant for too long, and though I wanted to feel connected to human beings again, I had this fight-or-flight response: "Get me out of here!" I remember being in a group of people I had really missed, but all I could feel was anxiety inching up my spine. I wanted to literally leave, not say goodbye, and just be home in my room, safe and solo.

In other social situations, I was totally tuned out, which I now know has its own fancy psychological term: disassociation. It's kind of like having an out-of-body experience, where I felt like I was watching myself go through the motions while I was somewhere else because, mentally, I was. Gradually, I got used to being around people again. It just took time, patience, and Anthony and my dad standing by me in case I freaked and started to bolt. It was such a weird feeling because all I said for months was, "I can't wait till this is over! I can't wait to see my friends and be back living my life again." Then, when I finally could, I flipped out. My dad said it was like I was opening the shades in a dark room and letting the light in. It was so bright I couldn't see, and it was really uncomfortable. I guess I needed time for my eyes to adjust, or maybe I just needed a cool pair of shades?

Pandemic aside, being a teen is tough. For starters, we have homework, tests, extracurriculars, dating, peer pressure, parent pressure, college applications, and oh yeah, virtually no sleep. Plus, everything is naturally amplified in our still-developing brains. Sometimes, I wish I could be a little kid again with nothing to worry about—no responsibilities and no way of knowing how messed up the world can be. With everything being so unsettled and uncertain these days, I'm tired of all the brain strain, you know? I am constantly turning things over and over in my mind, overanalyzing everything. *Why is this happening? Why do I feel like this? What will go wrong next?* So many questions I wish I could answer, but I can't. If life at this moment was a pre-calc pop quiz, I'd fail. But here is one thing I *do* know: all of the above can add up to one big mental health headache, and you can't ignore it. Push it down and it will come bobbing back to the surface.

When I sat down to write this book, I had one clear goal in mind: make publicly talking about mental health unscary. I wanted to fight the stigma and fear around mental health and help make it nothing to hide from. There is nothing—I repeat, *nothing*—to be ashamed of if you are feeling off-balance, out of sorts, or in over your head. I have learned that anxiety can manifest in so many ways, depending on the individual. For me, it becomes a need to turn inward, to shut the world out and take cover like a turtle hiding in its shell. Some people may feel explosive anger or hyped-up anxiety, while others freeze in their tracks. I've had friends describe stress as feeling paralyzed or glued to the spot. Some have scary thoughts that haunt their days and dreams. Others worry about anything they can't control. There's no wrong or right way to react, it's just how you process pain and distress. We all have to figure out what anxiety looks like for us, and how to cope with it, so it doesn't overshadow everything else.

What I want you to know is I have been there, and I am still there. I have good days and bad days and days when I just want to lie in bed, see no one, and not even check my phone. When one of those rolls around, I allow myself to experience it and I don't push it away. I tell myself, *This is the one bad day you're allowed this month. Take it and then shake it.* My friend Charli confessed to me that she has panic attacks—a really scary, heart-racing, can't-catch-your-breath sensation. She's working on it and

I'm proud of her for that, and also for sharing it with me publicly on my show. Her sister, Dixie, also admitted on her IG that she's dealt with anxiety and depression, and at times, her mind "just isn't in the right place." I guess we all feel things differently and have to search for the right fix for us. What I want to do is give mental health issues a voice so we can begin to break them down and work on them together.

How do you start? I think the best way is to come clean: "My name is Avani and my mental health is hurting!" I guess when I first started being more open about it, I worried people would judge or hold it against me. I didn't want to seem "broken," but I figured if millions of followers were going to see my life anyways, why not just let them see *all* of it? I didn't want to fake it anymore. I didn't want to pretend to be this happy-go-lucky girl if that wasn't my mood or mentality. Faking it is exhausting and wrong. I'm not sure why mental health tends to be an off-limits topic or makes people so uncomfortable. Here are some not-so-fun facts for you: According to NAMI (the National Alliance on Mental Illness), 75 percent of mental illnesses reveal themselves before age 24, and 50 percent show first signs before age 14. Also, according to experts, one out of five young people is dealing with some form of mental illness. What does that mean? That a lot of us are feeling it, and it needs to come out of the shadows.

Why then do so many of us, me included, keep mental health issues buried deep inside? What's the reason for holding back? I can speak from experience here: there are many. For starters: fear of being judged, labeled, or canceled. I seriously stressed about someone commenting on a post that I was "crazy," "dramatic," or "problematic." I didn't want to be a trending topic on some gossip site. Then I thought I was somehow "disappointing" my family, my team, or my fans by admitting I had a problem that wouldn't go away. Along with that, I didn't want to be a burden or put those around me on edge. The last thing I wanted was for my mom or Anthony to be walking on eggshells, afraid to upset me. I also thought admitting I was struggling would be like announcing, "Hey! Look at me! I'm a failure!" All my success and productivity seemed to hinge on my ability to perform at the top of my game. If I couldn't do that, what did that say about my career? What did it mean for my future?

But covering things up led me to a place where I didn't feel like myself anymore. I haven't been officially diagnosed, but I struggle with attention deficit. I can't stay focused on any one topic for more than a couple of minutes. I was in the process of getting tested in Indiana right before moving to LA, and then the pandemic happened. I deal with it, it's a part of me, and it should give you a clue as to where my crazy sense of humor comes from. When I made the difficult choice to open up about my mental health, I knew it wasn't just going to be to my inner circle, but to the world as a whole. I talked a lot about mental health on my show and asked doctors, experts, and real kids to weigh in. It was eye-opening. I learned that denying it won't make the problem go away. I learned that staying mentally healthy is just as important as staying physically healthy. If you get sick with the flu, you drink tea and honey, take a Tylenol, and have chicken soup. Isn't your brain worthy of some TLC when it's not feeling its best? Most important, I learned that you can gain insight into your own mental health by hearing the experiences of others. Sharing is caring, bebes. After I discussed mental health on my show, I was overwhelmed with support. So many people commented, "Me too!" and that empowered me. It showed me that I could use my platform to make a difference in a big way. I could get through to people who were hurting like I was. I could kickstart the conversation and let all of you take it to the next level. I could take a negative and turn it around into a positive to propel me forward. I'd be lying if I continued to let you think that nothing gets to me, 'cause it does. That's when I remind myself I have been through this before and I'm still here, still kicking. That's proof positive that this will blow over and be history one day. Chalk up another one on the scoreboard: Life 0, Avani 1.

Being a public person, I get a lot of people reaching out to ask for my advice. Every time that happens, it's like a switch goes off in my head and I want to help. But advice is one thing, fixing someone else is taking it too far. I could tell you what I would do, but who am I to say what will work for you? Mental health isn't one-size-fits-all. You have to do the work, and all anyone can give you, myself included, are the tools to fix yourself. So, with that in mind, let me say that I am a great listener. And you being here, reading these words on these pages, that's you listening to me. I appreciate it more than you know because it's freeing me up to acknowledge what I'm going through. If you're in the midst of figuring out your mess, what I can tell you has *really* helped me figure out mine is being honest with myself. My go-to reaction used to be to duck and cover, but now I am putting it out there in black and white for everyone to read. It's a big step for me to share what I've gone through and am going through. As little as a year ago, I would have been too terrified to spill. I would have just closed the book on this topic before I ever started writing it. But if my story helps someone, resonates with them, or encourages them to reach out to get the help they need, then I'm happy. Did you hear what I said? H-A-P-P-Y. Imagine that.

Run It Back: If You're Unhappy and You Know It...

+ Don't keep it to yourself. I know, easier said than done. You don't want to worry your parents, scare off your friends, or make people think you're messed up. I don't know anyone whose life is totally unproblematic, so you're in good company. It might be hard for people to hear it, but it's even harder for you to keep it bottled up. It feels so good to be real, give voice to my mental struggles, and get people thinking and talking about their own. It's like this huge weight is lifted and I can finally focus on healing instead of hiding. Yay me.

+ Distract yourself. I will literally sit and watch cartoons for hours with Anthony, cracking myself up. We will watch a new movie or cartoon every night: *Adventure Time*, *Steven Universe*, *The Amazing World of Gumball*, *Family Guy*, *Rick and Morty*, *Big City Greens*, *Gravity Falls*, *Uncle Grandpa*, *Phineas and Ferb*, *Bob's Burgers*, *The Simpsons*, *Clarence*, *The Regular Show*, *Sanjay and Craig*, and so many more. I think we might've watched every single cartoon and kids' show that there is (we're definitely trying). It's really hard to be sad when you're laughing so hard you can hardly breathe. I also recommend reading a book, listening to music, dancing around your living room, or challenging your siblings to a game of Fortnite. You get the picture: take your mind off your misery.

✦ Separate the sadness. The fancy term for that is "compartmentalizing." It means you don't let your upset invade every single nook and cranny of your daily life. If it's related to a relationship, keep it there instead of letting it take over your time for studying. If it's school-related, leave it behind when your classes wrap because it doesn't belong in your dance studio. Compartmentalizing is literally taking a mental break when you need it, and it works wonders.

✦ Make someone's day. Giving back is a great pick-me-up. I have all these boxes of unused makeup and I've finally decided it's time to go through them and donate them to an organization in LA that helps women who are getting back into the workplace. Studies have shown that helping others makes you feel better about yourself and your situation. Plus, it makes the world a whole lot better.

✦ Things change. My mom likes to rub my back and tell me, "Voni, this too shall pass." She's right. Stuff may suck at the moment, but it can and will get better. How do I know? Because I've seen it in action. What shook me to my core six months ago doesn't bother me all that much anymore. Even if the situation stays the same, your feelings can shift, especially when you've had some space to breathe and think it through. I have to remind myself of this constantly since I seem to attract drama like a magnet. The crisis I'm in will blow over, die down, and vanish into thin air. Just knowing that makes me hopeful, and hope is a great healer.

✦ TLC yourself. I see nothing wrong with a little retail therapy, binge-watching sesh, or long bubble bath. You deserve it, especially when you're not feeling your usual fabulous self. Make it a day that's "All about Me, Me, Me." It's not being indulgent; it's simply offering self-care to someone (YOU!) who needs to recognize how special they are.

✦ Write it down. Break out your journal and put those feelings down on paper. It's like an instant stress release—take it from the girl who just wrote herself 200-plus pages in this book! Every time I put my sadness or fear into words, it was like they were no longer a part of me. I set them free. Even if you're not the greatest writer, I highly recommend a little literary send-off for your troubles. Who knows, you could be the next great novelist and never even know it.

✦ Get help. If you can't talk to someone close to you, there are so many great groups and help-lines ready and waiting to give you emotional support. Don't hesitate if you're hurting. Connect, talk, and get some relief. Here are a few organizations to check out:

https://teenlineonline.org

https://www.imalive.org

https://suicidepreventionlifeline.org

On Avani

*M*y friend Riley Hubatka says:

I had been on TikTok for about a month when Amelie Zilber DM'd me: "I think we would be such great friends." She introduced me to Avani and put me in a group chat with the two of them. We would talk every single day and we made plans for me to come visit them. The first time I actually met Avani was December 2019. It was my very first time coming to LA. I live in Charlotte, North Carolina, and I was going to be in LA for only about three days to get some work done, but Avani insisted, "I want to see you. I want to meet you. I want to hang out." I spent the entire first day with her and we just clicked right off the bat. We went out to dinner and were able to be ourselves, not scared or shy with each other. It came so easily.

That's where it all started, and now we're like sisters. We text constantly throughout the day, and not even about important stuff. We'll just ramble and talk about stupid things and make jokes and send each other memes. Every time I go to LA, it's like I never left. We have such a great relationship and we're very, very close, even if we're across the country from each other.

We have these cute little nicknames: she calls me Dad and I call her Sugar Mama. When this pandemic calms down, we can't wait to go out to eat at Pink Taco on Sunset, where we used to hang a lot.

We make a lot of videos together for TikTok. Even if we never post them, we have dozens of funny drafts that we keep to ourselves. Although we have a very similar sense of humor, we're quite different in our emotions. Avani tends to get sad and cry a lot, and I tend to not show my feelings at all. It's definitely something she's been working on, being more open. We actually help each other a lot because she brings out the emotional side in me and I'm able to help her when she's down. I'll say, "It's just a season of life. You're going to get through it," and she'll tell me, "Hey, it's okay to cry. I've been there. We'll get through it together."

I'm constantly in awe of Avani's confidence. Not only does she wear whatever she wants, but she's confident in who she is as a person. She knows her morals and her values, and she sticks to them. She's not going to let anybody tell her who she can and cannot be, which is absolutely amazing. She's also incredibly kindhearted and sensitive to what other people are feeling. She loves so, so hard, and that is something that I genuinely love about her. Avani is fiercely determined in everything that she does. When she sets her mind to something, she won't rest until she gets it done. Once she starts something, she has to finish it. I'm a big procrastinator, so that's the complete opposite of me, which is another reason I look up to her.

Avani and I have the type of friendship where we're able to sit down and laugh about stupid things. If you were to listen in to our conversation, none of it would make any sense. But to us, it makes perfect sense because it's the Avani and Riley show! I'm so grateful I have this girl in my life. I don't know what I would do without her.

chapter twelve

Joy

*F*or me, joy is so much more than being in a good mood. It's a sensation that everything is right in the world and nothing can bring me down. It's the ultimate vibe. Finding that sweet spot in my feels doesn't happen too often, but when it does, it's like I'm wearing rose-colored glasses and the world is a big, beautiful place bursting with positivity. Think Willy Wonka's candy garden and you get a sense of what I'm saying: sunshine and lollipops (let's leave the Oompa Loompas out of it). The dictionary definition is "a feeling of great pleasure." But I think that's dumbing it down a little, don't you? Joy is more than that. It runs deep. You can be happy in the moment, but joy is all-encompassing and totally sweeps you up and away. Happiness shows on your face, but joy lives in your heart.

A lot of things make me happy: being with my boyfriend, doing fun things with friends and family, helping others, and painting on an amazing makeup look or drawing. But each of these things is fleeting. Anthony might leave for a while to hang out with his bros and I might wipe all my makeup off. When this happens, the momentary fun is over, and that can cause me to sink back into my blues. I think joy is longer lasting and purposeful. It's an adrenaline rush, a thrill that comes from the fact that you truly, madly, deeply love something or someone. Joy is rainbow vibrant, an explosion of feel-good vibes. It can come from small things or big life changes and milestones. It's all very personal. When you find it, you build on it, until one day it's just *there* and overflowing. Think of it like hitting the highest video game level on Monster Hunter World (my sis Priya came up with this analogy, so just go with it LMAO). You need to do quests, focus, go on missions where you rack up bounty and rewards. And after you've been grinding, you might just reach Master Rank. For the record, Priya is Master Rank 100, but it goes even higher. Joy is the same—you just want it to keep going and growing, and with each level there's potential for more. The way I see it, you have to keep collecting joy till you win the ultimate prize: a life that's rich in whatever your dreams are made of.

Having a good week of eating brings me joy because I know I'm supporting my health. Doing all my workouts for a week makes me *tired* but joyful because I can feel proud of my body. I get joy in completing all that I need to do in a day—checking off my list of reminders gives me a high. And occasionally, I get crazy amounts of joy out of splurging on a pair of sneakers. Sorry, but I'm a sneakerhead and I own it. The color purple is my happy color and anything in that shade brings me joy. My car is purple, the title of this book is written in purple, and ditto for the opening credits of my show. For our six-month anniversary, Anthony gave me a bouquet of purple forever roses and they sit by my TV so I can look at them every day. I post in a lot of purple LED lights because I love to bask in that violet glow.

Certain memories bring me joy, specifically when I finished and graduated high school online with an academic honors diploma. My mom and dad were so happy because they knew how hard it was for me to sit down, stay focused, and complete my schoolwork. I think of their faces in that moment and I feel all warm and fuzzy inside. When someone tells me that I'm doing well or I've accomplished something, that ups my joy quotient. Certain smells, too: I have this Versace perfume that I used in 2019. I wore it on dates with Anthony and on vacations, and I still have some left. Every time I take a whiff it reminds me that there was a time in my life when I was so insanely happy every single day and that can happen again. I also love the smell of popcorn because it means I'm either going to watch a movie or it's my rest time. Cartoons, kid movies, and rom-coms bring me joy. Looking at the huge pic of me and Anthony in front of my bed and printed on my blanket also does the trick.

For my aunt Hemali, cooking brings her tremendous joy. It's her act of creating something whole from individual ingredients, her art form as well as her gift to those she loves. It's a ritual that requires being mindful and present—no wonder some experts say it's great therapy for when you're feeling sad or anxious. For my aunt, it's not just *her* joy—we all get to experience those good vibes when we dig in. In this way, her cooking creates a sense of community because we all sit down at the table together and pass the plates, share stories of our day, connect. When she cooks, it's a demonstration of how much she cares; it's not just throwing stuff in a pot or pan, it's much more intimate than that. It's her expression of love for all of us, a way to affirm our bond as a family, and she puts great time and detail into every culinary creation. My mom says when you cook for someone you love, you're nourishing both their body and soul. I'm not the most skilled person in the kitchen, but when you put it like that, I'm willing to give it a try.

Recipes for Joy

DAD'S FAMOUS SPAGHETTI

My mouth waters whenever I smell my dad's famous spaghetti on the stove and garlic bread baking in the oven.

> 1 lb. lean ground beef
> 1 lb. Italian ground sausage
> 1 yellow bell pepper, diced
> 1 green bell pepper, diced
> 1 large Vidalia onion, diced
> 1 jar store-bought pasta sauce (Dad likes Italian
>   seasoning–flavored ones)
> 1 box spaghetti
> Pinch of salt
> Pinch of pepper
> Sprinkle of garlic powder to taste

Add the beef and sausage to a medium skillet, stirring until they're completely browned. Drain and set aside. In the same pan, sauté the peppers and onion until tender. Add the beef and sausage back to the vegetables. Next, add the pasta sauce. Combine and simmer for 10 minutes, adding salt, pepper, and garlic powder to taste. Meanwhile, cook the spaghetti noodles per package directions. Add the sauce to the spaghetti and serve with garlic bread.

DAL MOTH

I love to munch on this traditional Indian namkeen, a dry snack popular in North India and made from fried lentils, nuts, spices, and sev. This deep-fried, savory version comes from my aunt Hemali. You can find her on Instagram: @patelhemali and @HomemadeBy Hemali. She's also on TikTok: HomemadeByHemali. Aunt Hemali is an amazing cook with her own fans and followers—myself included, of course.

Soak overnight:

> 1 cup whole masoor dal
> Pinch baking soda (about ⅛ tsp.)
> Pinch of salt
> Pinch of turmeric powder

Spices:

> ½ tsp. red chili powder
> ½ tsp. chaat masala
> ½ tsp. powdered sugar
> ¼ tsp. black pepper
> ¼ tsp. cumin powder
> ¼ tsp. hing/asafoetida powder
> ¼ tsp. dried lemon powder

Salt to taste

Oil for deep-frying dal (a few inches' depth in a high-sided pot)

1 cup thin sev/fried gram noodles

1. After soaking dal overnight (about 8–10 hours), drain, rinse, place on a towel, and pat dry to remove as much liquid as possible.
2. Heat oil in a pan. Once hot, lower the heat to medium.
3. Fry dal in batches. Stir while frying so the dal doesn't stick together. You'll know it's ready when it floats to the surface. Remove fried dal to a bowl, then start the next batch.
4. Once all the dal is fried, add the spices and stir together.
5. Adjust salt and powdered sugar to taste.
6. Mix in the sev.
7. Once cooled, store in an airtight container.

CREAMY FRUIT SALAD

I love this healthy treat (another recipe from my aunt) for dessert or even for breakfast. You can boost the protein by using Greek yogurt instead of ice cream and mix in any fruit, seeds, or nuts you like, even mini marshmallows.

3 cups whole milk
½ cup sugar
1 cup softened vanilla ice cream
1 banana, chopped
1 apple, peeled and diced
1 pear, peeled and diced
½ cup seedless grapes, cut in half
¼ cup pomegranate seeds
Pinch of cardamom powder

1. Bring milk to a boil in a saucepan over low heat.
2. Add sugar and stir until dissolved. Let the boiled milk cool to room temperature.
3. Once cooled, add ice cream and stir until combined. Then add all the chopped fruits and pomegranate seeds and stir until combined.
4. Add cardamom powder and refrigerate until cold. Serve cold.

LOADED CHILI MAC

What happens when you mix two of my favorite dishes? You get the ultimate comfort food! Auntie nailed this one.

1 package elbow macaroni, cooked to package directions w/ 2 Tbsp. butter added after draining

1 lb. ground beef

1 onion, chopped

1 green bell pepper, chopped

3 fresh tomatoes, chopped

¼ cup fresh cilantro, chopped

3 garlic cloves, chopped

1 jalapeño, minced

1 package chili spice mix

1 can fire-roasted tomatoes, undrained

1 can fire-roasted corn, drained

1 can red kidney beans, drained and rinsed

1 can black beans, drained and rinsed

1 can broth (vegetable or chicken)

2 cups water (more if you like your chili soupy)

1 tbsp. sugar

Salt and black pepper to taste

1 cup sharp cheddar cheese, shredded or grated

Toppings:

Sour cream, shredded cheese, corn chips (such as Fritos), fresh cilantro, chopped onions, chopped jalapeños, crackers

Directions:

1. In a large skillet, brown ground beef, then drain.
2. Add onion, bell pepper, fresh tomatoes, cilantro, garlic, and chopped jalapeños to the ground beef and cook for 5 minutes.
3. Add chili spice mix and cook for 5 more minutes.
4. Add the canned tomatoes, corn, beans, broth, and water and cook for another 15 minutes on low heat.
5. Add sugar, salt, and black pepper to taste.
6. Add the cooked pasta and stir in cheese until melted.
7. Top with your choice of toppings.

PINEAPPLE UPSIDE-DOWN CAKE

This one looks so fancy, but it's actually really easy to make with a basic yellow cake mix. Pineapple Upside-Down Cake is one of my aunt's greatest hits and I always beg her to make it when we go back home to see her in Indy.

1 stick of butter
1 cup packed brown sugar
20-oz. can crushed pineapple packed in juice,
   drained (keep the juice)
1 package yellow cake mix
4 large eggs
Vegetable oil (according to cake mix directions)
Water (according to cake mix directions)

1. Preheat oven to 350 degrees.
2. In a 13" x 9" baking pan, melt the butter in the oven.
3. Once butter is melted, sprinkle the brown sugar over it.
4. Spoon the crushed pineapple on top of the brown sugar and butter.
5. Combine cake mix, eggs, and vegetable oil. For the amount of water called for in the cake mix instructions, use the reserved juice from the pineapple plus

as much water as you need to make up the total amount. Mix until a smooth batter is formed.

6. Pour the cake batter over the pineapple in the baking pan.

7. Bake for 40–45 minutes, or until a toothpick inserted in the center comes out clean.

8. Run a knife around the cake as soon as it comes out of the oven.

9. Let the cake cool for 5 minutes. Place a heatproof serving plate over the cake pan and CAREFULLY flip the cake over. Leave the pan on top of the serving plate for 5 minutes. Remove the cake pan and let the cake cool for 30 minutes before serving.

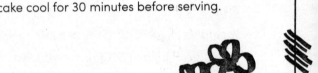

Run It Back: How to Find Everyday Joy

I love how joy resides in the little nooks and crannies of your daily life and, if you look carefully, you can always find it. My mom was raised in the Hindu culture, which believes that happiness stems from one's own actions—physical, mental, and spiritual. My dad is also big on the idea that you can claim your own joy if you just keep your eyes open to the world around you. He's very into reminding me to notice birds chirping, sunrises and sunsets, and the simple things that I might otherwise miss if I was too busy and couldn't be bothered. When you actually focus on being present, that's when joy jumps out and makes itself known. Think of joy as an adventure and go find yourself some—it will fill your day with a lot more light, laughter, and love. Here are a few good places to start:

◆ Share. I don't mean give someone half of your Snickers bar, but that's also a nice thing to do. I mean connect with people socially. It can be in person, over text, on FaceTime, in line at the supermarket checkout, or wherever. Personal connections make us happier, healthier, and generally feel better about our place in the world. I know when I'm in one of my moods, just talking to a friend or even a friendly stranger helps me feel less lonely. Sharing with you in this book has brought me so much joy that I never realized existed. What are you waiting for? Reach out and connect with someone—you'll thank me later.

✦ Review your joy. It's so much easier to find joy all the time if you can flash back to a moment when you felt joyful. So that's what it feels like! Keep a journal, make a list, or organize an album of "joy" photos on your phone. If you can recall what made you joyful in the past, it's that much easier to repeat it in the present.

✦ Fill your home with happy. I'm all about bright colors and surrounding myself with "stuff" that brings me joy. Photos, mementos, and thoughtful gifts Anthony has given me. I proudly display them rather than putting them away in a closet or drawer. I want to see them on the daily and be reminded of some of the best times of my life. I love for my room to be a vibrant, creative, energizing place—my own little heavenly spot. You don't have to do a major redecorating job; just pin a few pics to your bulletin board, pick up some cheap throw pillows in your fav colors, and create some mood lighting with LEDs or candles. Give your space a little sprucing up and watch the joy just flow right in.

+ Get moving. I know, exercise, ugh. There are days when it's the absolute last thing I feel like doing, but being present in my body, working my muscles, and filling my lungs with oxygen does help me feel joyful. It gets my heart pumping and makes me feel so alive. I also applaud my-self every time I get through a workout: "Good for you, Avani, you burned off that Happy Meal from lunch!" There's something about feeling the burn that brings me joy—the knowledge that I'm strong, powerful, and capable of pushing myself.

+ Look in little places. Joy doesn't always have to hang around life's biggest milestones and mo-ments. Sometimes, it likes ordinary spots, too. Like inside your morning cup of coffee, your little sister's laugh, that spot right behind your dog's ears where he loves to be scratched. Savor these everyday events and be mindful of each second that puts a smile on your face. Don't know 'bout you, but I'm feelin' it!

✦ Count your blessings. Acknowledge everything you're grateful for, big and small. It's hard to be unhappy when you're checking off a list of all the good stuff going on. Ever since I was a toddler, my parents have been reminding me to say "thank you." Now I know why. It's a good practice to spend just five minutes speaking aloud or writing out what you're grateful for, either right when you wake up or right before bed. It can be what you're grateful for in general or today; the point is to remind yourself how great you've got it and build off the positive vibe.

✦ Free your mind. It's hard to find joy when there's so much noise and clutter between your ears. Zone out to some music, meditate, or take a power nap—whatever you need to get rid of all the brain drain and find clarity. I've learned to make this part of my daily schedule, no matter how busy I am or how much I've got on my plate. For a few minutes, it can wait. Joy is calling.

On Avani

My aunt Hemali Patel says:

Avani is so special because she is strong-minded and does what she wants, no matter what. She doesn't let others deter her from her goals and dreams. My funniest memory of Avani is when she won the first place overall title at her very first gymnastics meet. She was so tiny, but already such a force! To see this itty-bitty girl standing up there with all those medals around her neck—I was afraid she would topple over.

When Avani was here in Indy, some of her favorite things I made were my homemade chili, pineapple upside-down cake, pastas, and desserts. She isn't afraid of spicy food, which is a good thing because Indian food has tons of spice. Avani loves it, even when everyone else's mouth is on fire.

I have learned many things from Avani about social media. I have learned what makes some videos better than others, how to get better angles, how to not let anyone bring you down with their negativity, and how to have fun while creating content. She also shows our whole family how to be considerate of everyone when posting. I'm really proud to be her aunt.

chapter thirteen

Face Time

*B*y now, I hope you've come to realize that everything I do has some underlying meaning. I never just randomly throw something out there; it always has a backstory. Same goes for my makeup line. When Morphe approached me about a collab, I shrieked in excitement. Literally, top of my bucket list: my own makeup collection. I think they were expecting me to just show up at a meeting and listen to their ideas or brainstorm, but I had the whole thing already plotted and planned out. I had sketches, Pantone chips, and a full-on mood board. I laid out the colors, the box design, the vibe (playful and edgy), the shade names, and even asked if they could imprint my drawings onto each of the pan colors and feature them on the packaging as well. "That's incredible!" They praised me: "We don't usually get people who are so organized and creative. You did all the work for us!"

Did I ever. I threw myself into it, creating something very personal. If this was going to be my collection, it was never going to be in name only. It had to be me down to every detail, and I got a little obsessed over it. I named the big main palette "For the Bebs" because I wanted my followers to know they were top of mind while I was thinking through all this. The collection has thirty bright colors because, as you know, I don't do dull or small. I literally sat there with the colors in front of me, racking my brain to figure out what I would call them.

A Who's Who of Makeup

The shades are named after friends and family.

Madi: "Madi don't like"

Charli: "Chunkin's coffee"

Lydia: "Lydster"

Anthony: "Anfony" (his fave color is blue, so I gave it to him)

Dad: "L-dawg" (what I call my dad when he's trying to be cool)

Shanti: "ShantiG"

Priya: "Pri-pri"

My dogs: "Jack&Benny"

My fam: "Gretals" (how we jokingly refer to our-selves, a combo of Gregg plus Patel, my mom's maiden name)

My cuz: "Sonia" (named for my cousin, who was the first person who taught me how to do my makeup)

Mom: "Mama's fav" (an evergreen shade that's my mom's favorite color)

Me: "my fav" (of course, a power purple)

"gymnast mems" (a shout-out to my former career, coaches, and teammates)

 *Avani-speak:*

"LMAO," "bruh," and "*star emoji*" are things I put in my comments and texts way too often. "Lilpapivoni" is my Twitter name.

"inaudible noise" is this funny sound my dad makes. We constantly call him out for it, so it had to be in there.

"diet" is for my fav drink, Diet Coke.

"u mad?" is what people used to comment when I started putting up evil clown faces on my feed. I was like, "No, I'm not," but I found it funny.

"beep boop" is the name of this little troll that my friend gave me. It used to be in all my TikTok comedy videos.

"clown" and "2016" are my greatest hit and my best year ever.

"seaweed" is named for my fav snack.

"fishy" is a word that Seb started up on our trip to the Bahamas. We all have sweatshirts that say "Bahamas Squad" on them, and on the hood it says "fishy." I'll give Sebastian creds for it.

Run It Back: Coming Clean

aking off my makeup is kind of a complicated process. I have sensitive skin, so I need to be gentle but not leave any product behind to clog my pores. Basically, here's how it goes, should you decide to do your own fierce face (and remember that you should always make sure you don't use any makeup or remover with ingredients you are allergic to or have sensitivities to):

✦ Latex and face putty usually peel right off, so that's where I start. You may have to wipe gently with an oil-based remover if adhesive, fake blood, or waterproof makeup is involved. Apply with a cotton pad and make sure not to leave any of the glue or goo behind. Hopefully, you've avoided your eyebrows because . . . ouch.

✦ I use cleansing balm to take off the face paint. It has oils and emollients to break down makeup, and it's usually a solid that melts into an oil once it warms up on your skin. Add water and it turns milky, but really breaks everything down. Vaseline also works wonders—it's light and lubricating, so makeup slides right off without too much irritation.

✦ If you applied glitter, it gets everywhere, and I usually find it stuck to my skin for days. Try using a cotton pad to apply baby oil or coconut oil in a sweeping motion. Don't rub hard—that stuff is rough!

✦ When you're done taking it all off, don't forget to moisturize. After all the application and removal, your skin needs to rehydrate.

✦ Give your skin a break. Doing too many looks in one day—even though you want to create content—can cause too much damage. I try and space mine out and go a day or two without makeup so my face has time to recover.

On Avani

My cousin Sonia Patel says:

I was the very first person to teach Avani how to do makeup! We were around thirteen and fourteen at the time. She would come over to my house and I remember she loved looking at all my makeup and swatching stuff. She started being more curious about it once she saw all the different products I had. She would try out all the different palettes, blushers, and lipsticks; we would do makeup looks on each other; and then we would wipe them off. We would keep working on each other's faces until it was time for her to go home. Neither of us knew anything about makeup. I think she thought I knew what I was doing but, looking back, I didn't have a clue. We have both improved a whole lot since then, but she has blown past me.

Avani is such a down-to-earth person. She's honest, funny, and one of the realest people I know. I have a million favorite memories of growing up together, but my favorite thing we used to do was thrifting. We would spend the entire day hitting all the thrift stores around our town. Anytime I would go thrifting with her, our car would be completely filled with bags of all the stuff we bought!

Avani has definitely grown a lot in the past few years, but I don't think she has changed. She is still the same nice and funny girl I grew up with and whenever I visit her it feels exactly the same between us. The secret to her success is simple: she works hard for what she wants, she's persistent, and she doesn't give up.

On Avani

My friend Sebastian Topete says:

I met Avani when she first came to LA—it was either her first night or her second night here, and she was staying at Madi's house. I knew of her, I guess, and we had talked a little online before she was local. My first impression? She was kinda shy. But I think you can say that of most people who are new to LA. It can be very overwhelming. She warmed up pretty quick, and I realized how genuinely funny she is. Like, the best sense of humor! We went to the Bahamas on spring break with a bunch of friends and it was literally the best vacation of my life. I do remember one really weird thing that happened. We were just there to have fun and relax, and this mob of fans was waiting for us in the lobby of the hotel. We didn't post anything on social media about where we were, so we had no idea how they figured it out and found us. We had to make a run for it like rock stars with security and we were cracking up. I also remember fans trying to sneak into our private villas, and us laughing in disbelief. I mean, none of us think of ourselves as famous, especially not Avani. She's just the most normal person, caring and friendly to anyone she meets. Before Corona hit, we went to Disneyland and acted like little kids there. It's been hard not seeing each other so often, not being able to travel, but we're hangin' in, waiting for stuff to open up again. The thing is, we can Snap each other and stay close till that time comes around. I just know there will be a lot more great memories made.

chapter fourteen

Action!

*I*n the fall of 2019, Brat TV reached out to me about an acting role they thought I would be perfect for: a new character named Gemma on the sixth season of *Chicken Girls*. Okay, I had never acted before, but I figured they knew what they were doing. Brat is a digital media network that makes original series on YouTube, and they have almost 5 million subscribers. They'd seen my content and thought the character was right up my alley. I was in LA at the time, staying with my manager, Erika, and it was smack in the middle of my prime Hype days. I didn't really have a lot of time to spare, but acting was always something that had interested me. I act in my videos, but that's just a few seconds. This would be ten episodes and I'd be appearing in most of them. It sounded like a lot of work, but also a lot of fun. Who wouldn't want to see themselves on-screen? Maybe I would love it, be good at it, and decide it was a career I wanted to pursue besides social media. Only one way to find out, right? I said yes.

I didn't actually have to audition. Casting just had me read some lines to get a feel for my acting abilities. When I didn't totally suck, they confirmed that I had the part. That's when reality set in. All of this sounded great, but I had no clue what I was doing. I didn't know anyone on the show, and TBH, I was so crazy busy I didn't have time to study up on seasons one through five. I relied on the director and the rest of the cast to get me up to speed. Everyone was welcoming and eager to answer any questions I had: "What exactly is a green room and why isn't it green?" "What's crafty?" FYI, it's short for craft services, which caters our meals on set. Most important, "What's the Wi-Fi password?" There was also a ton of technical lingo to learn. When the hair and makeup team double-checked us before the cameras started rolling, they would shout, "Last looks!" When it was time for me to transfer from school to set, the production assistant would say into her headset, "Avani walking!" and usher me over to the assistant director. Sometimes, I would scratch my head because filming was like a foreign-language immersion and I struggled to understand it at first. But it was also so exciting to see magic being made. I'd never seen a real clapboard before, and now my episode name and scene were written on it. The other thing that was completely surprising was how long it could take to wrap a two- to three-minute scene. Four pages in the script could take as long as four hours to shoot, depending on how complicated they were. How many angles? How many extra actors? Did it require intricate lighting, fog, or other effects? Sometimes we would shoot the same dialogue over and over because the director had to get me from the front, back, and in profile. When you're watching it on YouTube, it all goes by so quickly, but that little eleven-minute episode probably took us a week or more to nail. So much goes into making it all look so effortless.

Season six was a big one for *Chicken Girls*—lots of makeups, breakups, departures, and drama. Gemma contributes to that—she's pretty problematic. Besides causing bad feelings between Rhyme (Jules LeBlanc), who she picks to be on the cheer squad, and Quinn (Riley Lewis), who she doesn't, Miss Cheer Captain likes to stir up trouble. She starts off looking the part of a preppy cheerleader, but by episode two we start to see her true colors: she dresses in a tank top, flannel shirt, ripped jeans, and combat boots. "Let me guess," I ask Rhyme, "you're wondering why I'm a cheerleader when I'm dressed like I could be in an indie band?" We learn that my character's mom encouraged her to "try anything at least once." So Gemma tried cheer and the next thing she knew, she was captain (what, like it's hard?) and (another plot twist!) don't write her off as dumb because she's been accepted to Yale. So, let's just recap: she's smart, she's edgy, and oh yeah, she could care less what people think: "People who judge me in this outfit are on the sidelines." I loved that scripting because it sounded like something I might say to a hater. As the season progresses, Gemma takes Rhyme, an inexperienced sophomore, under her wing, inviting her to play Spin the Bottle at a party, sneak into an 18+ club with a fake ID, and ditch her Chicken Girls for a new, older, cooler crowd. When Rhyme spots her making out with someone who is definitely *not* her BF, Benji, Gemma threatens, "If you want to stay on this team, you're gonna learn to mind your own business." So, let's rewind. Here's the scoop on that kissing scene at The Spot. It was very weird, because I didn't know Jake Ambrose, the actor playing Anthony. He seemed like a perfectly nice guy, but he was older, and this wasn't his first rodeo. I, on the other hand, was about to shoot my very first make-out scene *ever*. My grandparents would be watching this when it aired. Awkward! Thankfully, *my* Anthony and I weren't dating just yet. We were friends and getting to know each other, so he didn't really care or hold it against me. Honestly, he probably doesn't even remember me mentioning it, but now that I brought it up, I'm sure he'll go back and watch season six just to check it out. The thing that they don't tell you about on-camera romantic scenes is how unromantic they really are—it's all so technical. Did we get it from all angles? Was the lighting good? Can we try it again with more of her face showing? Also, it's over before you know it. I remember planting one on the dude and the director yelling "Cut!" before I could even process what had just happened. Really? That's it?

Filming was very new and unfamiliar to me. There were parts of Gemma's personality that I couldn't relate to, like when she threatens Rhyme or cheats on Benji. That is stuff I would never do, but I had to make it seem real, because acting is being someone who isn't you. I would constantly ask myself, "What is Gemma thinking here? Why would she feel that way?" I would literally close my eyes and try to step into her shoes and react as if I were her in that moment. It can be really challenging, but also exciting. How often do you get to switch places with someone? When do you ever get to make believe when you're no longer a little kid anymore?

I also talked with the director about my character's motivation—where she was coming from and how she would say the line. We did a practice run before each scene and he often gave me feedback like, "Try it this way, maybe a little tougher." They gave me the entire season's scripts ahead of filming, so I had a clear picture of Gemma's endgame. She's definitely a manipulator and mean girl, but as Rhyme points out, she's just trying to make herself feel better. Gemma may talk and act like nothing and no one gets to her, but there's a lot of insecurity there. My theory is that she saw a little of herself in Rhyme and that might have felt threatening. Rhyme had the skills and the heart and could take Gemma's place one day. Still, I love that Gemma found herself at the end of the season, offered to help Rhyme get into a gymnastics camp, and learned from her mistakes. But I have to say, even when she acted like a baddie, Gemma's confidence made me happy. She was fierce and I would have hated to play someone who didn't have a backbone. Some of her costumes were kind of alien to me—you will rarely see me in dresses or skirts—but, thankfully, I didn't have a lot of costume changes. Gemma's cheer look got repeated often. The hair and makeup were very basic and didn't take too long—wild curly hair, natural makeup, and a ponytail, of course. Most of our scenes were shot at Brat Studios, but we did get to go on location at a school for a day, which was fun. I was shocked by how much of Attaway High and the town is actually on a studio lot that's built up to look like real classrooms, hallways, and even Rhyme's bedroom.

Learning my lines was very hard because I have the worst memory ever. I would think I knew them, but then they would fly right out of my brain. The other actors were very helpful and the director would cut my scenes into shorter segments so I was able to study lines before shooting again. My very first scene was with Jules, who I didn't know coming into the show, but we became good friends. She's an amazing person, such a pro.

Beyond acting, I had to attend school on set every shoot day. I did not enjoy this part of the job. I would shoot for an hour and be done, but I couldn't leave because I had to log three hours of school. Every moment I wasn't filming, they were throwing me back into "class," during which a tutor supervises and you can't talk. The irony was that I hadn't been in a real classroom in a long time since all of my assignments were through online school and could be done at my leisure. It didn't matter, though, because at sixteen I was expected to be studying three hours a day, regardless of what else I had going on. I found the whole thing ridiculous, but I guess when you're a teen actor you have to play by the rules. What kept me going was the knowledge that in just a few hours, I was going to see Anthony. I could sit through endless math equations if I knew he was waiting at the other end of the tunnel!

If I were to watch my episodes back today, I'd probably cringe because I was so young and green! It was only two years ago, but it feels like an eternity. However, it did prove to me that acting is something I want to pursue. I want to take more acting classes so I can become more skilled at it. I was doing it for a while, but (yet again) the pandemic and all the mental stress associated with it cut those plans short. Not to worry, I will be back. Being on *Chicken Girls* was my chance to take part in the process of filming and see if I had it in me. I'd say the answer is a definite yes.

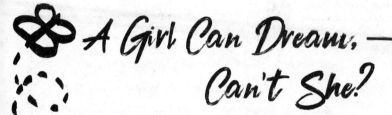

A Girl Can Dream, Can't She?

*I*f I could pick any role and any costar, here's what and who I'd choose!

✦ I am obsessed with the TV series *Euphoria*. I love it with my whole heart. I could totally see myself acting in an edgy drama like that, and I would love to work with any of the girls on the show: Zendaya, Hunter Schafer, Maude Apatow, Barbie Ferreira, Alexa Demie, and Storm Reid. They're the most talented cast I have ever seen and everything from the script to the makeup is goals.

✦ My ultimate leading man would have to be my boyfriend, Anthony (duh!). But if he was unavailable, I would settle for Leonardo DiCaprio circa the nineties. You know, the way he looked in *Titanic*, *Romeo + Juliet*, and *The Quick and the Dead*. I wouldn't mind filming a rom-com with him—it's only acting, after all. 😉

✦ If I was doing a buddy film, I'd have to choose my bae Riley Hubatka to play my best friend, especially if it was a comedy, because she is just hilarious, spontaneous, and would keep me laughing the entire time. Second choice: I think it would be pretty amazing to act opposite Alexa Demie, who plays Maddie on *Euphoria*. Her acting is flawless.

Run It Back: Could You Be an Actor?

*I*f you're asking yourself whether acting is something you want to do, too, here's what you need to know (full disclosure) before you decide:

✦ Acting takes sacrifice. It's not all red carpets, limos, and dressing up. It's hard work, long hours, and it comes with a steep learning curve. Ask yourself why you want to go into this profession. If you think it's to be rich and famous, think again. Most actors never win an Oscar or have a steady income, at least not in the beginning. You have to be willing to pay your dues, wait tables, be an extra, whatever it takes. You may have to do something else, something not so fun or exciting, until a big break comes along (if it comes at all). So be ready to cancel plans on friends because you need to study lines, film a self-taped audition, or go to an acting class. Also, be willing to have a backup plan that can support you while you audition. My dad always tells me that hard work pays off. Here's to hoping!

✦ Acting takes imagination. Can you picture your-self as someone else? Can you leave your own life behind and morph into another? This is my favorite part of acting—the ability to step into an-other person's shoes and take a stroll around. It's literally channeling a character so that you can become them in an authentic, believable way. When I played Gemma, I *was* Gemma. I thought like her and reacted like she would, given what I knew of her backstory. I can't think of anything cooler than getting hired to pretend.

✦ Acting takes patience. There aren't many over-night sensations in Hollywood. Accept that get-ting anywhere as a pro actor will take time, commitment, and a stubborn refusal to give up on your dreams. You will also spend lots of hours auditioning, waiting in the green room, and sitting in school on set. I can't sit still very long, so this is where I need the most practice, but it comes with the territory. If I want to be an actor, I can't expect insta-fame or insta-success. It's a nice idea, but it's not gonna happen.

✦ Acting takes studying. I know, that was a hard one for me to swallow, too. But you will have to learn lots of lines, work with acting coaches, and even research your role or the time period during which your project is set. What I will tell you is this: it gets easier. The first time I saw the *Chicken Girls* scripts and highlighted every sentence I needed to memorize, I freaked. I thought, *What did I get myself into?* But I broke it down into smaller segments and made sure that my director knew I was struggling. My castmates were always happy to run lines because it helped me to hear how they sounded when spoken. Everyone was really nice about it and, little by little, I got better and didn't flub my lines or forget which way I was supposed to walk down the hall.

✦ Acting isn't all about you. When you're part of a cast, it's a group effort, with everyone (hopefully) checking their egos at the door and coming together to create something great. It's no wonder that so many actors consider the cast and crew family. It truly feels that way because you spend more time together than you do with your own family. I also felt really humbled and grateful to be around a group who had grown up in their roles. You can't walk into an audition or set thinking you're better than everyone else. I'm all for confidence, but not when it steps on people in the process. Be kind, be cool, and be a team player.

chapter fifteen

Afterthoughts

*H*ere I am at the end of my book. Let's just take a minute to absorb this: "The End." It took me several months to get to this place, and I don't mean emailing the manuscript to my editor. I mean that I feel like I'm a different person who has gone through so much soul-searching, shape-shifting, and up-heaval while trying to make sense of it all on paper! Yet, here I am—standing, surviving, and killin' it. Applause, please, I made it! Just like graduating from high school, it's a huge milestone for me and a lot went into it.

Think about what the year 2020 brought, not just for me, but for all of us. I saw my plans evaporate. I was isolated from my friends, my grandparents, and the world in general. When-ever I poked my head out for some air, I freaked out or got criti-cized for not "taking the pandemic seriously." Oh, I took it seriously. It scared me and sent me running to a place of sadness, fear, and insecurity. My mental health took a nosedive. It's hard to be optimistic about anything when you have no idea what is going to happen next. My parents wanted to tell me everything would be okay, but they didn't know that for sure and they didn't want to make promises they couldn't keep. We just hung in and slowly but surely, things started to calm down. I kept posting on my socials, I filmed my show, I did photo shoots, and I sat in on creative meetings via Zoom. I've come this far and it's soon to be further.

I feel like I'm not just a year older, it's like I've aged a decade LOL. I feel a little old and tired sometimes from just having to *deal*, but I'm also wiser and stronger for it. As I write this, the world is still on shaky ground. We're all hanging our hopes on a new day and waiting for things to pick up where they left off. Did I mention that patience is not one of my strong suits? I have found these past several months so frustrating and so freakin' annoying. But, like I named my show, I'm here for it (all of it) because I don't think you can ever know what the good looks like unless you have the bad to compare it to. On my IG feed, I captioned one of the pics: "I could really use a good reboot, reset, refresh." I think we all could and I am holding on to the hope that one day soon, I can hug every one of you, see you face-to-face, and thank you for sticking by me. I am where I am and what I am because you believe in me and listen to what I have to say. This book is just that—thank you for stopping by!

I've done a deep dive into my past, acknowledged my present, and now (here we go!) I'm ready to do some gazing into my crystal ball so I can see the future. I don't think small. I see myself doing more fashion looks, maybe planning or launching my own line. I'm going to be working with more affordable brands because they speak to my thrifting spirit. I don't believe something has to be expensive to be cool. I want to teach people how to express themselves fearlessly through fashion and get creative with it.

I want to continue to act. That's always been a dream of

mine, and I got a small taste of it when I filmed *Chicken Girls*, but I see movies in my future and think I could do drama as well as comedy. I would love to get the chance to flex those muscles a little. Stay tuned.

Beyond that, hmmm . . . I suppose I should keep my options open, right? I'm a planner, so I'm not a fan of leaving things up in the air but, sometimes, you can be happily surprised by what comes your way. I'm just trying to spend some time sitting in the unknown. You can always be prepared for the worst, but don't forget to hope for the best. I don't need to have my entire future laid out in front of me; I can leave some things open to chance. It's like when colleges ask you to decide your major when you're applying. How do you know? How do you have a clear picture of where you'll be one year, two years, or four years from now? If you do, that's great and highly impressive—some people just know they want to be a veterinarian from birth. I thought I wanted to be a gymnast, but we saw how that turned out. Things can change in the blink of an eye. Didn't we learn that from the pandemic as well? Isn't it better to just roll with it, trust the universe, stop fighting the uncertainty, and see it as an opportunity for something awesome to arise? Kind of like when I go thrifting: I have no idea what I might find, but that's the excitement. It could be great, it could be not-so-great, but there's always a possibility that something really valuable might come of it.

Writing this book also taught me to release my fear. Certain situations will always scare me, but jumping into this one got me out of my comfort zone and showed me I don't have to be afraid to tell my truth. I'm really excited for everyone I know and have known to read about the real me. I think it will definitely change some minds.

But let's be real here: I'm eighteen. I'm still learning and figuring stuff out, and I've got a whole lot of living to do. One day, I might look back on all of this and wonder, *What in the world was I thinking?* And that's okay. I hope I keep growing and reevaluating what matters to me. If all this has been a small part of what I do with the rest of my life, then I'm cool with it. It's a snapshot of the girl I was on the way to becoming the woman I will be, and I gotta say, I kinda like her. She's a little weird, a little opinionated and stubborn, but she grows on you. So yes, it's "The End" but it's really "The Beginning." See you around.

Run It Back: What's Your A.Q. (Avani Quotient)?

Since graduating online high school, I have not been missing all those quizzes and tests. But not all of them have to be brain-busting, right? Why not take one for fun, all about me? I'm kinda curious to know if you were really paying attention (if not, don't worry—I'm an easy grader!).

1. The nickname my family calls me is:
   - ❏ Von Gretal
   - ❏ Sugar Daddy
   - ❏ Voni

2. My two dogs are named:
   - ❏ Jack and Benny
   - ❏ Ben and Jerry
   - ❏ Beb and Bebe

3. I *first* met my BF Anthony:
   - ❏ online
   - ❏ in line at a meet/greet
   - ❏ at a flea market, thrifting

4. My very first Clown Girl face:
   - ❏ had black oozing out of her mouth

❏ had purple skin
❏ had stars around her eyes

5. My favorite snack to eat is:
❏ seaweed
❏ black licorice
❏ avocado pudding

6. If it wasn't called Hype, our social house might have been known as:
❏ House of Olympus
❏ the Baddie House
❏ House of Charli

7. One of the best gifts Anthony has ever gotten me was:
❏ a giant cookie with his face on it
❏ Louis Vuitton sneakers
❏ purple forever roses

8. If I were stranded on a desert island, the one thing I could NOT live without is:
❏ my eyebrow tweezer
❏ my *Ren & Stimpy* DVD collection
❏ Diet Coke

9. I have NOT been bullied for:
❏ my purple car
❏ wearing a shirt that says "World's Greatest Grandpa"
❏ being a TikTok star

10. I have NOT been on vacay to:

   ❏ Hawaii

   ❏ Bahamas

   ❏ Paris

ANSWERS:

1. Voni; 2. Jack and Benny; 3. online; 4. had stars around her eyes; 5. seaweed; 6. House of Olympus; 7. purple forever roses; 8. Diet Coke; 9. wearing a shirt that says "World's Greatest Grandpa"; 10. Paris

If you got 8+ answers correct: Congrats! You're an Avani expert. You probably know more about me than I do LMAO. Anthony is not at all threatened. Okay, maybe just a little . . .

If you got 6–8 answers correct: You might have missed a few details while reading, but I won't hold it against you. I'm not sure if my two sisters could have scored 100 percent, but there's only one way to find out!

If you got 5 or fewer correct: Have we met? Just kiddin'! Go back through the book and see if you can learn some more about me—and yourself while you're at it. It's worth extra-credit points!

On Avani

*L*ast words: What is the one word that comes to mind when you think of me?

Nessa Barrett: Passionate (and wifey!)

Madi Monroe: Hilarious

Benji Krol: Philocaly

Charli D'Amelio: Talented

Riley Hubatka: Kind

Seb Topete: Fishy (JK!) Caring

Krissy Saleh: Extraordinary

Lydia Pettersson: Real

Chase Keith: Catnoir

Anthony Reeves: Mine

Acknowledgments

I had no idea what it would take to write a book. There was no way I could have done it by myself. I wouldn't have had enough words to fill up a page if it weren't for everyone who has been in my life in some way, shape, or form. I'm overwhelmed by all the love and support I've received. I want everyone to know I did not go through any part of my life alone, and I would not be here today without my friends and family.

To my parents, thank you just doesn't seem enough. Your unlimited love and support have made me feel like I can accomplish anything. I will forever be grateful for all of the sacrifices you made just so I could achieve my dreams.

Shanti and Priya, well, what can I say? I am very blessed to have you as my sisters.

Anthony . . . my beb, my happy person, and my everything.

To my closest friends, Riley, Lydia, Madi, and Charli. You have been my crutch through all this. Thank you for being there when I needed it and for making me laugh to the point of losing my breath.

Dixie, Seb, Nessa, Chase Keith, Bryant, Krissy, Katie, Gracie, Rowan (to name a few): it is amazing to have friends who truly care about me!

I want to thank Chase Hudson, Thomas Petrou, and everyone at the Hype House for welcoming me into the Hype family.

Thank you to my grandparents (Ba and Dada) for staying on top of my schooling. Pop-Pop: thanks for giving love and laughter to the family . . . we love you, RIP. Thank you to Aunt

Hemali for always feeding me and spoiling me for no reason. Sonia, my third sister, thanks for getting me started on makeup.

To my coaches Eric and Tracy: thanks for always believing in me and pushing me to be my best. To all my gymnastics teammates: thanks for all the support and awesome memories.

My incredible manager, Erika Monroe-Williams, thank you for everything that you have done, not only for me but also for my family. You have been my mentor, my friend, and my manager. I am so grateful to have you in my corner.

To my management—Marienor Madrilejo, Keith Bielory, Rebecca Rusheen, Matt Luyber, and Julia Perez—THANK YOU for all the countless hours and hard work that you've put into Team Avani!

To the best PR team, Charlene Young and Stephen Huvane, thank you for always fighting for me and getting me nothing but the best. We have had an amazing year so far and I can't wait to see what the future has in store.

I want to thank Ryan Goodell and his legal team at Morris and Yorn for having my back, always.

To my team at Gallery Books, thank you so much for helping me make my book dream a reality. Sheryl Berk, thank you for taking the time to help me tell the story of my life. Jeremie Ruby-Strauss, Andrew Nguyen, and Molly Gregory, you made it all so easy! Also many thanks to Jen Bergstrom, Jen Long, Aimee Bell, Sally Marvin, Steve Breslin, Lisa Litwack, Chelsea McGuckin, Caroline Pallotta, Jen Robinson, and Abby Zidle.

I want to say a huge thank-you to all the brands that gave me the opportunity to work with them. Thank you for trusting me with your products.

Finally, my bebs, all the people behind the screens, I appreciate you more than words can say. You call yourselves my fans, but I consider you my friends. Thank you for believing in everything I do. Thank you for always checking in on me and making me feel like a real human. I most definitely wouldn't be in the position I am in now without you. I love you, bebs.

About the Author

Avani Gregg is a digital creator, social media personality, actress, and self-taught makeup artist. Gregg has a reach of more than fifty million highly engaged followers—winning her the 2019 Shorty Award for TikToker of the Year and a spot on the *Forbes* 30 Under 30: Social Media list.